WHY
STUDY
HISTORY?

REFLECTING ON THE
IMPORTANCE OF THE PAST

JOHN FEA

Baker Academic
a division of Baker Publishing Group
Grand Rapids, Michigan

Published by Baker Academic
a division of Baker Publishing Group
P.O. Box 6287, Grand Rapids, MI 49516-6287
www.bakeracademic.com

Printed in the United States of America

Library of Congress Cataloging-in-Publication Data
Fea, John.
    Why study history? : reflecting on the importance of the past / John Fea.
        pages cm
    Includes bibliographical references and index.
    ISBN 978-0-8010-3965-2 (pbk.)
    1. History—Religious aspects—Christianity. I. Title.
BR115.H5F43 2013
907.1—dc23
                                                            2013015201

In keeping with biblical principles of creation stewardship, Baker Publishing Group advocates the responsible use of our natural resources. As a member of the Green Press Initiative, our company uses recycled paper when possible. The text paper of this book is composed in part of post-consumer waste.

13   14   15   16   17   18   19   7   6   5   4   3   2   1

Contents

Acknowledgments

As always, I owe a great debt of gratitude to my students. Much of what I have written here has been forged through conversations—in the classroom and out—with the bright young minds that come to Messiah College to study history. I dedicate this book to them. My Messiah College undergraduate research assistants continue to shine. Tara Anderson, Natalie Burack, and Amanda Mylin tracked down books and articles, making my research much easier. Katie Garland not only provided invaluable research support, but she also assembled the original book proposal. She is well on her way to a stellar career as a public historian. Megan Sullivan edited the page proofs. Upon hearing Megan reading the manuscript aloud in a room adjacent to my office, I realized that my thoughts on historical thinking had become a book. The students enrolled in my "Introduction to History" and "Historical Methods" classes in fall 2012 read drafts of several chapters and discussed them with me in class.

I have presented my ever-evolving thoughts on the importance of historical thinking to several audiences over the past few years. Thanks to the Messiah College history department (where I delivered the inaugural Faith and History Lecture in 2010), the Center for Applied Christian Ethics at Wheaton College (especially its director, Vince Bacote), the Center for Vision and Values at Grove City College (especially Paul Kemeny and Steven Jones), and St. Peter's United Methodist Church in Ocean City, New Jersey (especially pastor Brian Roberts) for the invitations to speak. Jay Green of Covenant College provided helpful remarks on an earlier version of chapter 7. I am also grateful to the history faculty at Woodberry Forest School who provided stimulating conversation on many of the ideas covered in this book and to the hundreds of history teachers across the nation with whom I have had the privilege of sharing my thoughts on historical thinking through my work with the Gilder-Lehrman Institute of American History.

Thanks to *Touchstone* magazine for permission to adapt parts of chapter 4 from my essay "Thirty Years of Light and Glory" and to Jared Burkholder, David Cramer, and Pickwick Press for permission to borrow material for chapter 7 from an essay I wrote in *The Activist Impulse: Essays on the Intersection of Evangelicalism and Anabaptism.*

My family, as always, has been supportive of my writing and historical work. Carmine Fea offered me a week at her house in the north woods of New Hampshire that allowed me to complete the first draft of this book. My parents, John and Joan Fea, remain curious and encouraging about all of my projects. And Joy, Allyson, and Caroline (who promised me a Reese's Peanut Butter Cup when I finished the last two thousand words) continue to remind me what is most important in life.

Prologue

EVERY FALL I WALK INTO A LARGE LECTURE HALL FILLED with students for the first day of History 141: United States History Survey to 1865. Over the years, this course has become the bread and butter of my job as an American history professor. Students enroll in it to fulfill a "general education" requirement, and thus, for many of them, it will be the only history course that they take during their four-year college experience. A large percentage of them do not want to be there. They would rather be taking a more specialized course in their individual majors. But from where I stand in the cavernous surroundings of the tiered classroom, I realize that this will be the only chance I get to convince them that the study of history is important to their lives as citizens, Christians, and humans. My approach to the course is something akin to evangelism. Every now and then, I will get a convert—a student who decides to become a full-fledged history major—but in the end I am happy if, at the end of the semester, students have developed an appreciation for the past and how it has shaped their lives.

For many history professors in American colleges and universities, the United States survey course is something to avoid. They prefer to teach advanced classes in their areas of expertise. These courses take them out of the lecture hall and into the seminar room, complete with its long table and more relaxed atmosphere. Such courses are populated not by students trying to fulfill a general education requirement but by the advanced history majors who have signed up for the class presumably out of a love for the subject. These kinds of courses are fun to teach, but History 141 remains my favorite. If for whatever reason I could no longer teach it, my pedagogical life would be less satisfying. I guess you could say that I am more of an evangelist and a preacher than a pastor and teacher.

A few Septembers ago I was chatting informally with a first-year student about how he was adjusting to his initial week of college classes. He observed that every professor in every course he was taking spent the first or second day of the semester delivering what he called a "What Is" lecture. After probing some more, I realized that the student had coined this phrase to describe the lecture that most professors give to general education students to introduce them to a particular field of study. This student said he had just sat through a week of lectures with titles such as "What Is Physics?," "What Is Sociology?," and "What Is Philosophy?" If you are a professor, I am sure you know exactly what this student meant. In History 141, I always devote some time to a "What Is History?" lecture. During this lecture, I get my students acquainted with the basics of the field, such as the difference between a primary and secondary source, the meaning of the word *historiography*, and the ways historians practice their craft. I talk briefly about how the past speaks to the present and how it is also a foreign country, where people tend to do things differently than we do today. And since I am a Christian who teaches history at a Christian college, I get the privilege of exploring questions about the integration of faith and historical thinking. What kinds of resources are available in the Christian tradition to help us gain a better understanding of the past? What is "providential history," and why will it not play a role in the course?

Sometimes I leave the lecture hall after the "What Is History?" lecture frustrated. I only have fifty minutes to make my pitch, and though I know that the meaning of history will come up again as we move through the course material for the semester, I wish I had the time to develop my thoughts more fully. This book is a response to my frustration. I hope you will read this book as an extended "What Is History?" lecture—a primer on the study of the past. My primary audience for the book is Christian college students who are studying history, but much of what I have to say is applicable to history students with other religious affiliations or none at all and history students (or buffs) of any age. I also hope the book will be a resource for graduate students and college professors, especially those who are just starting to get their feet wet in the classroom or who are in the process of developing their own "What Is History?" lectures. Scholars, and especially those who specialize in historiography or the philosophy of history, will not find much that is new in this text, but I do think I have organized the material in a way that might prove useful for teaching.

I have deliberately made an effort to blend the theoretical and the practical in jargon-free, easily accessible prose. Much of the scholarly work in historiography is so impregnable to the undergraduate mind that I am afraid it turns students off to the discipline. While I have not avoided complex ideas at the intersection of history and theory, I have largely downplayed them in favor of an approach that students will find useful. I hope that readers will see the importance of thinking like a historian (chap. 1) and using the past responsibly in public life (chaps. 2 and 3). I have devoted considerable attention to the way Christians should think about the past (chaps. 4 and 5), how history can contribute to a healthy democratic society (chap. 6), how history can deepen our spiritual lives (chap. 7), and how the study of history prepares one for a variety of careers and vocations in an ever-growing and expanding marketplace (chap. 8). An epilogue contains some thoughts about how the study of history might enrich and strengthen the witness of the Christian church in the world. In the end, rather than writing a defense of historical knowledge against postmodern critiques or trying to decipher whether or not there is a distinctly "Christian" view of history, my focus is on the pursuit of history as a vocation.

I hope I am able to win some converts. Let's begin!

1

What Do Historians Do?

W HAT IS HISTORY? ANYONE WHO TYPES THIS QUESTION into an internet search engine will discover an array of answers. Henry Ford famously said, "All history is bunk." Voltaire, the eighteenth-century philosopher, believed that history is "the lie commonly agreed upon." The American satirist Ambrose Bierce wrote that history is "an account, mostly false, of events, mostly unimportant, which are brought about by rulers, mostly knaves, and soldiers, mostly fools." In a quote that warms the heart of many historians, the Irish writer Oscar Wilde said, "Anyone can make history; only a great man can write it." Are those who do not remember the past condemned to repeat it? The Spanish philosopher George Santayana thought so, and so do thousands of Americans when asked why students should study the subject. What is the purpose of studying history? What do historians do? Does everyone who conducts a serious study of the past qualify as a historian? "In my opinion," writes Pulitzer Prize–winning historian Gordon Wood, "not everyone who writes about the past is a historian. Sociologists, anthropologists, political

1

scientists, and economists frequently work in the past without really thinking historically."[1] What does Wood mean?

History and the Past

Any introductory conversation about the vocation of the historian must begin by making a distinction between "history" and "the past." Most average people think that these two terms are synonymous. They are not. The past is the past—a record of events that occurred in bygone eras. The past is dates, facts, and things that "happened." The past is what probably turned many of us off to the subject of history during our school years. Perhaps some of you may recall the economics teacher in the popular 1986 film *Ferris Bueller's Day Off*. This teacher reinforces a common stereotype, made famous by Arnold Toynbee, that history is little more than "one damn thing after another." Played brilliantly by actor Ben Stein, the teacher stands before the class in a tweed sport coat, tie, and thick glasses, rattles off details about the Hawley–Smoot Tariff Act and "voodoo economics," and monotonously asks his bored students to finish his sentences:

> In 1930, the Republican-controlled House of Representatives, in an effort to alleviate the effect of the . . . *anyone, anyone?* . . . the Great Depression, passed the . . . *anyone, anyone?* . . . the tariff bill, the Hawley–Smoot Tariff Act which . . . *anyone, anyone?* . . . *raised or lowered?* . . . raised tariffs in an effort to collect more revenue for the federal government. Did it work . . . *anyone, anyone?* . . . *Anyone know the effects?* . . . It did not work and the United States sunk deeper into the Great Depression.

This teacher, with his knowledge of certain facts about economic life in America, might be a successful candidate on *Jeopardy*, but he is not teaching history.

We all have a past. So do nations, communities, neighborhoods, and institutions. At times we can be reasonably sure about what

1. Gordon S. Wood, *The Purpose of the Past: Reflections on the Uses of History* (New York: Penguin, 2008), 276.

happened in the past. We know, for example, that the Battle of Lexington and Concord took place on April 19, 1775, or that Islamic terrorists attacked the first tower of the World Trade Center in New York City at 8:46 a.m. on September 11, 2001. But at other times, as the chronological distance from a particular moment in the past grows greater, our memory starts to fail us. Sometimes the documentary or oral evidence that tells us what happened in the past is limited or untrustworthy. Whatever the case, the past is gone. Yet we would be foolish to suggest that it has not had its way with us—shaping us, haunting us, defining us, motivating us, empowering us. Enter the historian.

History is a discipline. It is the art of reconstructing the past. As historian John Tosh writes, "All the resources of scholarship and all the historian's powers of imagination must be harnessed to the task of bringing the past to life—or *resurrecting* it."[2] The past is messy, but historians make sense of the mess by collecting evidence, making meaning of it, and marshaling it into some kind of discernible pattern.[3] History is an exciting act of interpretation—taking the facts of the past and weaving them into a compelling narrative. The historian works closely with the stuff that has been left behind—documents, oral testimony, objects—to make the past come alive. As John Arnold has noted, "The sources do not 'speak for themselves' and never have done [so]. . . . They come alive when the historian reanimates them. And although the sources are a beginning, the historian is present before or after, using skills and making choices. Why *this* document and not another? Why *these* charters and not those?"[4] There is a major difference between a work of history and a book of quotations.

Historians are always driven by the sources—they cannot make things up—but they do have power to shape their narratives in a style that might be described as "artistic." Too often I have heard

---

2. John Tosh, *The Pursuit of History*, 3rd ed. (New York: Longman, 2002), 7.

3. John Arnold, *History: A Very Short Introduction* (New York: Oxford University Press, 2000), 13; Arthur S. Link, "The Historian's Vocation," *Theology Today* 19 (April 1962): 78.

4. Arnold, *History*, 77.

historians describe their work entirely in terms of research. They spend years in the archives combing ancient records, and once the research is complete, they describe the next phase of the historical task as "writing it up." This phrase implies that they will simply translate their research into prose form without paying any attention to the literary quality of what they are "writing up." Anyone who has read a scholarly history journal knows what I mean. This problem is not new. In 1939 historian Allen Nevins, a strong advocate of making history accessible to general audiences, said, "The worst examples of how history should never be written can be discovered in past files of *American Historical Review*."[5] (The *American Historical Review* was, and continues to be, the most important scholarly history journal in the world.) Such an approach to doing history is common when writing an academic paper, a master's thesis, or a doctoral dissertation, but too often the bad habits learned in graduate school stay with historians as they enter their professional careers. In the 1990s an academic journal staged an annual "Bad Writing Contest." One of the winning entries came from a scholarly article about the history of American imperialism. Here is a taste:

> When interpreted from within the ideal space of the myth-symbol school, Americanist masterworks legitimized hegemonic understanding of American history expressively totalized in the metanarrative that had been reconstructed out of (or more accurately read into) these masterworks.[6]

While many historians *do* make an effort to write well, others do not. This is unfortunate because the effective and compelling dissemination of one's work is at the heart of the historian's vocation. Since the professionalization of history in the late nineteenth

5. Allen Nevins, "What's the Matter with History," *Saturday Review of Literature* 19 (February 4, 1939): 3–4, cited in Peter Novick, *That Noble Dream: The "Objectivity Question" and the American Historical Profession* (New York: Cambridge University Press, 1988), 196.

6. *Philosophy and Literature: The Bad Writing Contest*, denisdutton.com /bad_writing.htm, accessed June 14, 2012.

century (which we will discuss more fully in chap. 3), the literary quality of historical writing that defined an even earlier era has been largely lost, replaced by the accumulation of data and evidence in what professional historians call a "monograph."[7] While there is much to learn from the skills and practices of academic historians, and historical narratives build off of specialized research, this particular development in the history of the profession has been unfortunate. Whether it is through a book, article, website, exhibit, lecture, or lesson, all historians present their ideas to the public in some fashion and should do so in ways that are accessible.[8]

The best historians tell stories about the past—stories that have a beginning, a middle, and an end. Most stories end with a lesson or a "moral." While a historian may not explicitly preach the moral of his or her story, if told in a compelling fashion, the moral will always be evident to the reader. We use narratives to make sense of our world. It is how we bring order to our own human experiences and the human experiences of others. Jonathan Gottschall, in his recent *The Storytelling Animal: How Stories Make Us Human*, reminds us that the mind "yields helplessly to the suction of story."[9] If a quick glance at the *New York Times* best-seller list over the course of the last decade is any indication, the history books that have reached the largest audience are written by narrative historians. Writers such as David McCullough, Doris Kearns Goodwin, and the late Stephen Ambrose have brought the past alive to ordinary readers through their gifted prose and storytelling abilities. They have proved that a book about the past, in the hands of a skillful

7. Novick, *That Noble Dream*, 40.

8. Tosh, *Pursuit of History*, 141, 50.

9. Jonathan Gottschall, *The Storytelling Animal: How Stories Make Us Human* (New York: Houghton Mifflin Harcourt, 2012), 3. For a helpful analysis of Gottschall's work from the perspective of historical thinking, see Allen Mikaelian, "Historians vs. Evolution: New Book Explains Why Historians Might Have a Hard Time Reaching Wide Audiences, Getting a Date," *AHA Today* (blog), May 9, 2012, blog.historians.org/articles/1650/historians-vs-evolution-new-book -explains-why-historians-might-have-a-hard-time-reaching-wide-audiences -getting-a-date.

historian-writer, can be a page-turner. This is because, as historian William Cronon writes,

> As storytellers we commit ourselves to the task of judging the consequences of human actions, trying to understand the choices that confronted people whose lives we narrate so as to capture the full tumult of their world. In the dilemmas they faced we discover our own, and at the intersection of the two we locate the moral of the story. If our goal is to tell tales that make the past meaningful, then we cannot escape struggling over the values that define what meaning is.[10]

The Five C's of Historical Thinking

Historians are not mere storytellers. Not only do they have the responsibility of making sure that they get the story right; they are also charged with the task of analyzing and interpreting the past. In other words, they need to *think like historians*. Historians Thomas Andrews and Flannery Burke have boiled down the task of historical interpretation into what they call the "five C's of historical thinking."[11] I have found this introductory approach to historical thinking to be extremely helpful in teaching students how to go about their work as apprentice historians. According to Thomas Andrews and Flannery Burke, when doing their work, historians must always be sensitive to *change over time*, *context*, *causality*, *contingency*, and *complexity*. Let's explore these ideas more fully.

Historians chronicle *change over time*. While there is continuity between past eras and our own, there has also been significant change. For example, the United States changed considerably between 1776 and 1900: the meaning of the Constitution was defined more clearly by a bloody civil war; the demographic makeup of the country changed immensely with the arrival of new immigrants;

10. William Cronon, "A Place for Stories: Nature, History, and Narrative," *The Journal of American History* (March 1992): 1370.
11. Thomas Andrews and Flannery Burke, "What Does It Mean to Think Historically?," *AHA Perspectives* (January 2007), www.historians.org/Perspectives/issues/2007/0701/0701tea2.cfm.

and access to democratic practices, such as voting, was gradually applied to nonlandholders, African Americans, and women. Historians trace these changes. As we will see, their task is to take their audiences on a journey by shedding light on the ways in which life in past eras was different from the world in which we now live. I am writing this paragraph on July 27, 2012. Earlier this evening I watched, with billions of other people around the world, the opening ceremonies of the London Summer Olympic Games. Many of you will remember these ceremonies for the scene, crafted by film director Danny Boyle, in which James Bond and "Queen Elizabeth" parachuted into the Olympic stadium from a helicopter to the roaring applause of the British faithful. I was struck by the way Boyle's ceremony was based on the historical concept of change over time. The ceremony traced the movement of Great Britain from an agricultural society to an industrial society to a technological society. In essence, Boyle was delivering the world a very expensive and very elaborate history lesson. The historical task is inherently progressive because the historian is ever aware that things do not stay the same.

Historians think differently than others. When historians are confronted with a new development in contemporary life, their natural reaction is to wonder how such a development differs from previous developments. For example, historians might trace the process in which a town's Main Street went from a thriving economic center to a depressed area filled with abandoned storefronts that they now encounter. Or historians might ask how the United States moved from a society in which news was spread orally to a society in which more people find their news via the internet. Historians themselves work in the chronological space between the predominantly oral cultures of an earlier era and our present-day internet culture. As Wood has written, "The historian is to describe how people in the past move chronologically from A to B, with B always closer to us in time."[12]

Historians also study the past in *context*. First, historians, like any interpreters of documents and sources, analyze words in a

12. Wood, *Purpose of the Past*, 83.

given historical text as part of the message of the entire text. The context provides meaning. Politicians, for example, are often prone to ignore context when exploiting the words of their opponents for political gain. During the 2000 presidential primaries, Republican candidate George W. Bush's campaign produced an advertisement against his opponent John McCain that referenced a statement from McCain's hometown newspaper, *The Arizona Republic*. "It's time," the *Republic* stated, "that the rest of the nation learns about the McCain we know." Coming from Bush in the midst of a hotly contested political primary battle, most people from other parts of the country would have assumed that what the people of Arizona "knew" about McCain would somehow hurt his chances of winning the GOP nomination. But actually, Bush's campaign did not quote *The Arizona Republic* in context. The statement about McCain went on to say, "There is much there to admire. After all, we have supported McCain in his past runs for office."[13]

Another example of how the past can be distorted when not understood in context comes from Christian political activist David Barton, one of the nation's foremost supporters of the idea that the United States was founded as a "Christian nation." One of the staples of Barton's talks to churches around the country is the exhibition of an 1809 letter written from American founder and United States President John Adams to Benjamin Rush, a Philadelphia doctor and signer of the Declaration of Independence.[14] Barton is quick to call attention to a section of the letter in which Adams writes: "There is no Authority civil or religious: there can be no legitimate Government but what is administered by this Holy Ghost." This quote seems to support the idea that Adams was a Christian who believed that the third person of the Trinity was somehow responsible for the creation of the American republic.

13. John Broder, "The 2000 Campaign: The Ad Campaign, a Matter of Promises," *New York Times*, February 12, 2000, www.nytimes.com/2000/02/12/us/the-2000-campaign-the-ad-campaign-a-matter-of-promises.html.
14. John Adams to Benjamin Rush, December 21, 1809, in *Old Family Letters: Copied from the Originals of Alexander Biddle* (Philadelphia: J. B. Lippincott, 1892), A: 248–49.

But what Barton's audiences do not know is that he only reads part of the letter. A few sentences later, Adams makes it clear what he thinks about this notion that "there can be no legitimate Government but what is administered by this Holy Ghost." Adams writes, "All this is all Artifice and Cunning in the secret original of the heart, yet they all believe it so sincerely that they would lay down their Lives under the Ax of the fiery Fagot for it. Alas the poor weak ignorant Dupe human nature." In other words, Adams was being sarcastic. He was actually criticizing those who were foolish enough to believe that the Holy Spirit was in the business of establishing governments.[15] This kind of cherry-picking happens all the time, and it makes for the worst kind of historical interpretation.

Second, any event from the past should be understood in light of the circumstances, settings, or belief systems in which it occurred. This is especially the case when analyzing and narrating the history of ideas. The ideas of great thinkers, such as Plato or Thomas Aquinas or John Locke, are the products of the cultural worlds in which these men lived. Historians, as Peter Novick writes, are "loath to apply implicitly timeless criteria in judging what we describe and, historically, explain."[16] For example, it would be absurd to suggest that someone living in early America was a homosexual because they were described in a letter or diary as being "gay." The word *gay*, as most of us probably realize, was used very differently in the eighteenth century than it is commonly used today. Part of the historian's vocation is to debunk context-free explorations of the past by looking closely at the evidence, exploring the larger social and cultural context in which words are used, and exposing these fallacies to the general public. As we will see in chapter 3, the past can sometimes be akin to a foreign country where people do things differently. Historians must always keep in mind the culture and belief systems of this foreign country as they interpret their sources and draw conclusions about their meaning.

15. Gregg L. Frazer, *The Religious Beliefs of the American Founders* (Lawrence, KS: University of Kansas Press, 2012), 121.
16. Novick, *That Noble Dream*, 6.

Historians also realize that specific events in the past are best understood in relation to other events; in other words, historians are concerned with *causality*—the examination of cause and effect. In this sense, the historian moves beyond the mere recitation of facts and tries to explain why particular events happened in the way they did or how events have been shaped by previous events. What were the social, cultural, economic, or political factors that "caused" the American Civil War? How does the long history of slavery, segregation, and Jim Crow laws explain why the civil rights movement emerged when it did? What role did the immediate aftermath of World War I play in motivating Adolf Hitler to form the Nazi party? The historian uses the sequence of events in an attempt to determine causality.[17]

Because the past is removed from the present and because the human experience as it unfolds through time is so complex, it is often difficult to nail down definitive causes for many historical events. Take, for example, the case of the Umbrella Man. On November 22, 1963, the day John F. Kennedy was assassinated, the skies in Dallas were sunny and clear. Yet photos of Kennedy's motorcade route through the city reveal a man standing along the road with an open black umbrella, probably the only person with an open umbrella in all of Dallas that day. The man with the open umbrella was standing on Dealey Plaza near Kennedy's motorcade precisely at the time the gunshots were fired. What caused this man to stand under an open umbrella on a perfectly sunny Texas morning? It would seem natural, if not logical, to suspect that a man with an open umbrella standing at the spot of the assassination was somehow connected to the plot to kill the president. But when the Umbrella Man testified before the House of Representatives in 1978, he said that he stood under the umbrella to protest the World War II appeasement policies of Kennedy's father, Joseph Kennedy. (While Joseph Kennedy served as the United States ambassador to England in the 1930s, he supported the decision of British Prime Minister

17. Lee Benson and Cushing Strout, "Causation and the American Civil War: Two Appraisals," *History and Theory* 1 (1961): 163; Margaret MacMillan, *Dangerous Games: The Uses and Abuses of History* (New York: Modern Library, 2009), 38.

Neville Chamberlain to let Hitler conquer neighboring European countries unopposed. The strategy was called "appeasement," and Chamberlain—and Joseph Kennedy—thought it was the best way of stopping Hitler from continuing with his imperialistic romp through the continent.) The Umbrella Man said his umbrella was a reference to Chamberlain's famous black umbrella, an iconic symbol of his supposed weakness in the face of Hitler's advances.

For historians, the case of the Umbrella Man reminds us that there are an infinite number of explanations or potential causes for any historical event, even some that seem so weird or strange that they are virtually impossible to identify. So while historians should certainly try to explain the causes of historical events, they can never be entirely sure how one event may or may not have influenced another. Sometimes the actions of humans in the past do not conform to what we deem to be common or ordinary patterns of behavior. Sometimes we simply don't know.[18]

Historians are also concerned with *contingency*—the free will of humans to shape their own destinies. As historian David Hackett Fischer notes, people's choices matter. It is the historian's task to explain the way people are driven by a personal desire to break free from their circumstances and the social and cultural forces that hold them in place. History is thus told as a narrative—an often exciting and heroic one—of individual choices made by humans through time. Contingency, of course, is at odds with other potential ways of explaining human behavior in the past. Fatalism, determinism, and even Christian providentialism (which we discuss more fully in chap. 4) are philosophical or religious systems that teach that human behavior is controlled by forces—fate, the order of the universe, God—that are outside the control of humans. While few professional historians today would suggest that chance, determinism, or God's providence is a helpful way of interpreting past events, it is undeniable that we are all products of the macrolevel cultural or structural contexts that have shaped the world into which we

18. For the story of the Umbrella Man, see Errol Morris, "The Umbrella Man," *New York Times*, November 21, 2011, http://video.nytimes.com/video/2011/11/21/opinion/100000001183275/the-umbrella-man.html.

have been born. Karl Marx suggested that human action is always held in check by "the circumstances directly encountered, given, and transmitted from the past."[19] It is unlikely that any proponent of contingency would deny that human behavior is shaped by larger cultural forces, but in the end historians are in the business of explaining why people—as active human agents—have behaved in the past in the way that they did.

One prominent example of contingency is the way that historians of the Civil War have interpreted the Battle of Antietam. After suffering several defeats at the hands of the Confederacy, the Army of the Potomac (the main Northern army under the leadership of General George McClellan), desperate for a military victory, was preparing to meet the Army of Northern Virginia (under the command of Robert E. Lee) in a major military campaign, which would eventually take place at Antietam Creek in Maryland. About one week before the battle, while the Army of the Potomac was passing through Fredericksburg, Maryland, Corporal Barton Mitchell of the 27th Indiana Regiment found a copy of Lee's battle plans. There were seven copies of "Special Orders, No. 191" produced by the Army of Northern Virginia, and one of them was now in enemy hands. Historian James McPherson has suggested that the "odds against the occurrence of such a chain of events must have been a million to one," and "yet they happened." The Battle of Antietam turned out to be the bloodiest single day in American history. Over 6,300 soldiers were killed or mortally wounded. But the Union victory on September 17, 1862, prompted President Abraham Lincoln to issue the Emancipation Proclamation, freeing the slaves in the South and setting the war on a course that would eventually result in Northern victory.[20] And it was all because someone stumbled across a piece of paper rolled around three cigars lying in a field.

19. Karl Marx, *Eighteenth Brumaire of Louis Bonaparte* (1849), in *Karl Marx and Friedrich Engels: Selected Works* (New York: International Publishers, 1968), 97.
20. The best treatment of the battle is James McPherson, *Crossroads of Freedom: Antietam* (New York: Oxford University Press, 2002).

There are several ways that we can interpret what happened in the week leading up to the Battle of Antietam. Perhaps it was mere chance. Wheaton College English professor Roger Lundin is not entirely satisfied with this answer. He would prefer to see the theological dimensions of contingency. As a Christian drawing from the ideas of fifth-century theologian Augustine, Lundin questions whether a coincidence like this is ever possible:

> The history of a nation and the fate of a race dependent upon a piece of paper wrapped round a few cigars in a field? That sounds as uncannily coincidental and disturbingly unpredictable as the claim that a baby wrapped in swaddling clothes and lying in a manger could be the son of God. It is, apparently, a law of life that so much depends upon contingent events and the free actions of agents, both human and divine.[21]

Lundin wants to remind us that, for Christians, contingency gets us only so far. Humans have free will, but it is ultimately exercised in the context of a sovereign God who orders the affairs of his creation. As we will see in later chapters, the idea of God's providence in matters such as the Battle of Antietam is a subject worthy of exploration for Christians, but these kinds of theological matters are not part of the historian's job description.

Finally, historians realize that the past is *complex*. Human behavior does not easily conform to our present-day social, cultural, political, religious, or economic categories. Take Thomas Jefferson for example. Jefferson is the most complex personality of all of the so-called founding fathers. He was the primary author of the Declaration of Independence—the document that declared that we are "endowed by [our] Creator with certain unalienable Rights, that among these are Life, Liberty and the pursuit of Happiness." He was the author of the Virginia Statute for Religious Freedom—one of the greatest statements on religious freedom in the history of the world. He was a champion of education and founder of one

21. Roger Lundin, "Changing the Script," *Books and Culture*, July/August 2003, www.booksandculture.com/articles/2003/julaug/8.24.html?paging=off.

of our great public universities—the University of Virginia. As a politician, he defended the rights of the common man, and he staunchly opposed big and centralized governments that threatened individual liberties. As president, he doubled the size of the United States and made every effort to keep us out of war with Great Britain. At the same time, Jefferson was a slaveholder. Though he made several efforts to try to bring this institution to an end, he never succeeded. Jefferson needed his slaves to uphold the kind of Virginia planter lifestyle—complete with all its consumer goods and luxury items—that he could not live without. He was in constant debt. And he may have been the father of several children born to his slave Sally Hemings.

Another example of the complexity of the past is the ongoing debate over whether or not the United States was founded as a Christian nation. I recently published a book titled *Was America Founded as a Christian Nation?* In the course of my promotion for the book—at speaking engagements and on radio shows across the country—I was often asked how I answered this question. I found that most people came to my talks or tuned into my radio interviews with their minds already made up about the question, looking to me to provide them with historical evidence to strengthen their answers. When I told them that the role of religion in the founding of America was a complicated question that cannot be answered through sound bites, many people left the lecture hall or turned off the radio disappointed, because such an answer did not help them promote their political or religious cause. Yet the founding fathers' views on religion were complex, and they do not easily conform to our twenty-first-century agendas. The founding fathers made sure to keep God and Christianity out of the United States Constitution but did not hesitate to place distinctly Christian tests for office in most of the local state constitutions that they wrote in the wake of the American Revolution. Some founders upheld personal beliefs that conformed to historic orthodox Christian teaching, while others—especially major founders such as Adams, Jefferson, James Madison, and Benjamin Franklin—did not. The founders opposed an established church and defended religious liberty while at the same time suggesting that Christianity was essential to the health of the republic.[22]

The life of Jefferson and the debate over Christian America teach us that human experience is often too complex to categorize in easily identifiable boxes. The study of the past reminds us that when we put our confidence in people—whether they are in the past (such as the founding fathers) or the present—we are likely to be inspired by them, but we are just as likely to be disappointed by them. Sometimes great defenders of liberty held slaves, and political leaders who defended a moral republic rejected a belief in the resurrection of Jesus Christ or the inspiration of the Bible. Historians do their work amid the messiness of the past. Though they make efforts to simplify the mess, they are often left with irony, paradox, and mystery.

All Historians Are Revisionists

As noted above, the responsibility of the historian is to resurrect the past. Yet, because we live in the present, far removed from the events of the past, our ability to construct what happened in bygone eras is limited. This is why the doing of history requires an act of the imagination. Sometimes we do not have the sources to provide a complete picture of "what happened" at any given time. As historian Peter Hoffer notes, "History is impossible. Nothing I have written or could write will change that brute fact."[23] Or, in the words of historian David Lowenthal,

> No historical account can recover the totality of any past events, because their content is virtually infinite. The most detailed narrative incorporates only a minute fraction of even the relevant past; the sheer pastness of the past precludes its total reconstruction. . . . The

22. John Fea, *Was America Founded as a Christian Nation? A Historical Introduction* (Louisville: Westminster John Knox, 2011).

23. Peter Hoffer, *The Historian's Paradox: The Study of History in Our Time* (New York: New York University Press, 2008), 179.

historian must accept Herbert Butterfield's "tremendous truth—the impossibility of history."[24]

Historians must come to grips with the fact that they will never be able to provide a complete or thorough account of what happened in the past.

Even the best accounts of the past are open to change based on new evidence or the work of historians who approach a subject with a different lens of interpretation. In this sense, history is more about competing perceptions of the past than it is about nailing down a definitive account of a specific event or life. As Lowenthal notes, "History usually depends on someone else's eyes and voice: we see it through an interpreter who stands between past events and our apprehension of them."[25] While the past never changes, history changes all the time. Think, for example, about two eyewitness accounts of the same auto accident. Even if we can assume that the drivers involved in the accident believe that they are telling the truth about what happened, it is still likely that the police will receive two very different accounts of how the accident occurred and two different accounts of who is to blame or who *caused* the accident. It is thus up to the police officer in charge, or perhaps a judge, to weigh the evidence and come up with a plausible interpretation of this historical event. But let's imagine two weeks after the paperwork is filed and the case is closed, a reliable eyewitness to the accident emerges with new evidence to suggest that the person who the judge held responsible for the accident was actually not at fault. This new information leads to a new historical narrative of what happened. History has changed. This is called revisionism, and it is the lifeblood of the historical profession.

The word *revisionism* carries a negative connotation in American society because it is usually associated with changing true facts of the past in order to fit some kind of agenda in the present. But actually, the historian who is called a "revisionist" receives a high

---

24. David Lowenthal, *The Past Is a Foreign Country* (New York: Cambridge University Press, 1985), 214–15.
    25. Ibid., 216.

compliment. In his book *Who Owns History?*, Pulitzer Prize–winning history professor Eric Foner recalls a conversation with a *Newsweek* reporter who asked him, "When did historians stop relating facts and start all this revising of interpretations of the past?" Foner responded, "Around the time of Thucydides." (Thucydides is the Greek writer who is often credited with being one of the first historians in the West.)[26] Those who believe "revisionism" is a negative term often misunderstand the way it is used by historians. Revisionists are not in the business of changing the facts of history. Any good revisionist interpretation of history will be based on evidence—documents or other artifacts that people in the past left behind. This type of reconstruction of the past always takes place in community. We know whether a particular revision of the past is good because it is vetted by a community of historians. This is called peer review. When bad history does make it into print, we rely on the community of historians to call this to our attention through reviews.

A few examples might help illustrate what I mean when I say that revisionism is the lifeblood of history. Without revisionism, our understanding of racial relations in the American South after the Civil War would still be driven by what historians call the "Dunning School." William Dunning was an early twentieth-century historian who suggested that Reconstruction—the attempt to bring civil rights and voting rights to Southern blacks in the wake of the Civil War—was a mistake. The Northern Republicans who promoted Reconstruction and the various "carpetbaggers" who came to the South to start schools for blacks and work for racial integration destroyed the Southern way of life. In the end, however, the South did indeed rise again. In Dunning's portrayal, Southerners eventually rallied to overthrow this Northern invasion. They removed blacks from positions of power and established a regime of segregation that would last for much of the twentieth century. These so-called redeemers of Southern culture are the heroes of the

26. Eric Foner, *Who Owns History? Rethinking the Past in a Changing World* (New York: Hill and Wang, 2002), xvi.

Dunning School, an interpretation of Reconstruction that would inform D. W. Griffith's *Birth of a Nation* (1915), one of the most popular, and most racist, motion pictures of the early twentieth century. In the 1930s the Dunning School was challenged by a group of historians who began to interpret the period of Reconstruction from the perspective of the former slaves. Rather than viewing the blacks in the post–Civil War South as people without power, these revisionist authors provided a much richer understanding of the period that included a place for all historical actors, regardless of skin color or social standing, in the story of this important moment in American history.[27]

Similarly, in 1913 historian Charles Beard wrote a book titled *An Economic Interpretation of the Constitution of the United States*. Beard argued that the framers of the Constitution were motivated primarily by economic interests. The founders were all wealthy landholders and thus had a natural desire to protect their wealth from common farmers and smaller farmers who could conceivably threaten the founders' livelihood if they were given too much power in government. The Constitution was thus a "counter-revolution." With its system of checks and balances, and a Senate and President not elected directly by the people, the Constitution, according to Beard, curbed the democratic impulses of the masses and made it more difficult for them to pass legislation that would bring economic equality to the country. Beard's thesis was eventually challenged by revisionist historians who argued that the founders were motivated less by economic gain and more by political ideas. These revisionists, such as Bernard Bailyn and Gordon Wood, read hundreds of pamphlets written by the proponents of revolution and concluded that the founders and framers of the Constitution sought to apply the republican ideals of eighteenth-century writers who defended individual rights and liberties. In their effort to offer a different interpretation of the American founding period, one based more on ideas than class warfare, Beard's critics have given

27. Novick, *That Noble Dream*, 232. The most thorough critique of the Dunning School is Eric Foner, *Reconstruction: America's Unfinished Revolution, 1863–1877* (New York: Harper & Row, 1988).

us a more complete picture of why the founding fathers framed the Constitution the way they did.[28]

One of the more recent developments in the historical profession has been the way historians have turned to religion as a category of explanation. During the 1960s and 1970s, many publishers of American history textbooks responded to a host of Supreme Court decisions that limited religious expression in public schools. For example, in the wake of cases such as *Engel v. Vitale* (1962), which made any prayer in schools unconstitutional, and *Abington v. Schempp* (1963), which prohibited school-sponsored Bible reading, publishers began to downplay the role of religion in American history. Things got so absurd that several popular textbooks avoided the mention of religion in discussions of the Pilgrims and the Puritans. Scholars of the First Amendment have universally argued that many textbook companies, and their clients in the public schools, misunderstood these Supreme Court decisions to mean that religion was not permitted in the curriculum. Because they feared that schools would not purchase their books if they had too much religion in them, textbook companies chose instead to take religion out. After *Vitale* and *Schempp*, school districts and textbook companies became unnecessarily paranoid about violating the First Amendment's religious clause and thus erred on the side of caution.[29]

In the last several decades, revisionist historians have been correcting this problem. They are making religious belief and practice an important part of the stories that they are telling about the past. Historians are taking seriously the way religious faith shapes behavior. In fact, the membership statistics of the American Historical

28. Charles Beard, *An Economic Interpretation of the Constitution of the United States* (New York: Free Press, 1913). For revisionist challenges to Beard, see Forrest McDonald, *We the People: The Economic Origins of the Constitution* (Chicago: University of Chicago Press, 1958); Bernard Bailyn, *The Ideological Origins of the American Revolution* (Cambridge: Harvard University Press, 1967); and Gordon S. Wood, *The Creation of the American Republic, 1776–1787* (Chapel Hill: University of North Carolina Press, 1969).

29. Association for Supervision and Curriculum Development, "Religion in the Curriculum," *Journal of the American Academy of Religion* 55 (Fall 1987): 569–88.

Association, the largest and most important organization of professional historians in the country, reveal that religion is now the most popular subject being explored by practicing historians. American religious history is one of the hottest subfields in American history. While the Christian Right continues to complain about the apparent lack of religious content in textbooks, this revisionist revival promises to give faith a prominent place in the American history curriculum.

In the end, all historians are revisionists. The Christian historian R. G. Collingwood wrote that "every new generation must rewrite history in its own way; every new historian, not content with giving new answers to old questions, must revise the questions themselves." This may mean that a historian will challenge the cherished myths of a particular culture or uncover evidence that does not bode well for a patriotic view of one's country. (At other times, of course, evidence could strengthen the public bonds of citizenship.[30]) As new evidence emerges and historians discover new ways of bringing the past to their audiences in the present, interpretations of specific events change. This makes history an exciting and intellectually engaging discipline.

Is Historical Knowledge Possible?

If finding the whole truth about what happened in the past is nearly impossible and if interpretations of the past are constantly being changed or revised, then how can we make any definitive statements about what really happened in the past? In other words, is historical knowledge possible? For several decades, postmodernists have harshly criticized the narratives that historians tell about the past. A narrative, they argue, is ultimately shaped by a narrator who brings his or her biases to the story, exercises power over the

30. Collingwood quoted in John Lewis Gaddis, *The Landscape of History: How Historians Map the Past* (New York: Oxford University Press, 2002), 103–4. Also Joyce Appleby, Lynn Hunt, and Margaret Jacob, *Telling the Truth about History* (New York: W. W. Norton, 1994), 158–59; MacMillan, *Dangerous Games*, 43.

story, and chooses which voices to include in the story and which voices to exclude. Take, for example, a college history textbook. Many undergraduates assume that the textbook they have been assigned for their United States or World Civilization survey course simply provides them with a narrative of "what happened" in the past, without realizing that the authors of that textbook have made interpretive choices—either consciously or subconsciously—in how they have chosen the story. The authors have made choices about how much space to devote to certain historical actors, how the various pieces of the past are organized and presented, and where to begin and end the story. As a result, many postmodernists argue that no single narrative is capable of actually capturing the past because it will always be the product of the biases and interpretive choices (often based on those biases) that the narrator brings to the story. Narratives will thus be forever contested and do not offer us any reliable guide to what happened in the past. As Cronon notes, "The vision of history as an endless struggle among competing narratives and values may not seem very reassuring. How, for instance, are we to choose among the infinite stories that our different values seem capable of generating?"[31]

In the midst of this postmodern attack on historical narrative, several historians have stepped up to defend the discipline. Cronon, who as I write this is serving as the president of the American Historical Association, is not unwilling to abandon the "immense power of narrative writing," but he also insists on "defending the past . . . as real things to which our storytelling must somehow conform lest it cease being history altogether." Historical narratives, he argues, cannot contradict the "known facts of the past," and they must be written within a diverse community of historians who will expose our biases and correct our "wrong-headed" assumptions and interpretations. "Most practicing historians," Cronon argues, "do not believe that all stories about the past are equally good." The practice of deciphering what is a good story about the past, and what is not, comes

31. Cronon, "A Place for Stories," 1370.

through the historian's willingness to work within a fellowship of other historians who are also interested in defending the past. Cronon concludes, "There is something profoundly unsatisfying and ultimately self-deluding about an endless postmodernist deconstruction of texts that fails to ground itself in history, in community, in politics, and finally in the moral problem of living on earth."[32]

Others have used a similar defense of history against postmodernist critics. Historian John Arnold writes,

> To relinquish "Truth" and the idea of *one* history does not lead to absolute relativism, where any version of events is taken as being equally valid as any other. It does not, for example, give succor to those charlatans and ideologues who seek to deny that the Holocaust ever happened. The evidence for the systematic murder of more than six million people by the Nazis is overwhelming. To try to argue that it never occurred is to violate the voices of the past, to suppress that evidence which goes against that twisted thesis.[33]

Though the historical task is always limited by our distance from the past, historians must never cease in their pursuit of truth. History is not an exact science. Historians will never reach anything close to a modern certainty about everything that happened in a bygone era, but, as Joyce Appleby, Lynn Hunt, and Margaret Jacob have argued in *Telling the Truth about History*, this should not stop them from trying. A significant amount of historical knowledge can be ascertained through the diligent investigation of the sources available to us. When the historian's vocation to pursue truth is combined with the reality that we can never produce a complete account of the past, we get what Hoffer calls "the historian's paradox." History may be "impossible," but "something happened out there, long ago, and we have the ability, if we have the faith, to learn what that something is." Hoffer wants historians to know that

32. Ibid., 1371–74.
33. Arnold, *History*, 119.

it is safe to go back into the archives, safe to return to the classroom and the lecture hall, safe to sit at the word processor or to lift the pen over the yellow pad, safe to go to the library and take out a history book or buy one on Amazon.com. It is safe to teach and write and read and listen to history.[34]

Summing Up

This chapter has looked at the way people—from Henry Ford to George Santayana—have attempted to define the discipline of history. Historians think about the world differently than others. They tell stories about the past, but they also analyze and interpret what those stories mean and how those stories provide insight into the human experience as it has unfolded through time. If you are reading this book as part of a history course, take some time to listen to how your professor—a trained professional in historical thinking—explains the past. Notice how each lecture and discussion builds on the previous one ("change over time" and "causality"), how they include "complex" human characters acting in time to create a compelling story ("contingency"), and how these characters live in worlds that are often fundamentally different from our own ("context").

If you listen carefully, you may even hear your professor debunking commonly held myths about the past or explaining why this or that older view of the past cannot be sustained by the evidence he or she is presenting in the lecture or the primary document that you are reading. In the process, you will realize the redundancy of the term "revisionist history." Since the goal of historians is to explain, to the best of their ability, what happened in the past, history is always changing and historians are always revising. I also imagine that your professor's lectures assume that something actually happened in the past. In other words, they are doing their best to tell you stories that are true. As historian Shirley Mullen

34. Appleby, Hunt, and Jacob, *Telling the Truth about History*, 4, 181; Hoffer, *Historian's Paradox*, 181.

has written, historians "bear witness" to the past. They "are called upon to report what they have seen."[35] Such witness bearing should inspire you to action—to dive into the sources of the past, engage in the necessary detective work, and imaginatively tell stories that will remind our generation what it has meant to be human. A noble task indeed!

35. Shirley A. Mullen, "Between 'Romance' and 'True History': Historical Narrative and Truth Telling in a Postmodern Age," in *History and the Christian Historian*, ed. Ronald A. Wells (Grand Rapids: Eerdmans, 1998), 23–40.

2

In Search of a Usable Past

I T IS OUR NATURAL INSTINCT TO FIND SOMETHING USEFUL IN THE past. Recently a colleague in the education department at the college where I teach told me about a student teacher who was having a hard time making his history lesson relevant to the present needs of his pupils: "I told Sam that if history does not have relevance to our world today, then why study it? Why teach it?" On one level, my colleague gave Sam some good advice. If the past does not have any connection to the present, then what good is it? Why should students have to make sense of it? Many believe that if the past does not serve our needs in the present, whatever those needs might be, it is worthless. This chapter examines our never-ending quest for a past that is usable. It focuses on our natural inclination to make the past our own by consuming it. The consumption of the past is inevitable and can even be useful in making sense of our contemporary world, but, as we will see in chapter 3, it must always be done with caution.

A Consumable Past

As modern individuals we have an insatiable desire to consume. We need to consume to live. But we have also learned to be discriminating shoppers. We consume those things that meet our needs, and we ignore the rest. So it should not surprise us when we apply the same habits of consumption that we practice in the supermarket to the way we approach the past. As mentioned in the last chapter, the past is always with us. We are forced to come to grips with it. We have no choice but to consume it, to make meaning of it, and to make it usable in our lives. Americans are particularly good at consumption. It is part of our DNA. Whatever Thomas Jefferson meant in the Declaration of Independence by the inalienable right to the "pursuit of happiness," Americans have defined happiness largely in terms of individualism. During the nineteenth century, we created a culture that celebrated such individualism. Democracy, which was the equivalent of a political curse word to many of the founding fathers because it implied rule by uneducated people who were incapable of putting the needs of the country over their own, blossomed in an unrelenting fashion. By the 1830s, to quote historian Wilfred McClay, America became "a heroic fantasy of boundless individual potential, a vision of personal infinitude that impartially brushed aside the severe and impassible limits imposed by custom, history, and even . . . original sin."[1] All of the states in the Union had adopted a policy of universal manhood suffrage, empowering men to participate in the shaping of American society in unprecedented ways. With the opening of the West to settlers during this period, Americans could shape their own destinies, pursue happiness and independence through the acquisition of land, and make a better life for themselves and their families.

Similarly, with the rise of the market economy in the early nineteenth century, the United States became a consumer society. Capitalism thrives when manufacturers are successful in creating desire for the goods and products they make. It is an economic system that teaches us that the good life is obtained through the gratification of our lust for goods and commodities. In fact, it claims that indulgence in consumer products is a virtue because it

1. Wilfred M. McClay, *The Masterless: Self and Society in Modern America* (Chapel Hill: University of North Carolina Press, 1994), 42.

leads to further production which, in turn, stimulates the economy. (Think about George W. Bush, in the wake of the tragic events of September 11, 2001, telling Americans to go out and shop.) To quote Adam Smith, "The desire for food is limited in every man by the narrow capacity of the human stomach; but the desire of the conveniences and ornaments of building, dress, equipage, and household furniture, seems to have no limit or certain boundary." As one of the great architects of capitalism, Smith had a vision to build an economic system around these wants.

Both democracy and consumerism are directly linked to the greatest American value of all—progress. As citizens of the first nation formed during the Enlightenment, Americans have long been committed to the improvement of themselves and their society. To get elected in a democratic culture, politicians running for office must offer their constituencies a vision for moving society forward. Personal ambition and self-improvement have been at the heart of the American creed ever since Benjamin Franklin held up his own life, in the pages of his *Autobiography*, as an example of how to "make it" on these shores. American progress is tied to making our lives better by making our lives easier and more entertaining through consumption. In the United States, self reigns supreme.

What does all this mean for the study of history in our age? The French visitor to America Alexis de Tocqueville, writing in the 1830s, described the connection between American individualism and historical amnesia:

> Not only does democracy make men forget their ancestors, but also clouds their view of their descendants and isolates them from their contemporaries. Each man is forever thrown back on himself alone, and there is danger that he may be shut up in the solitude of his own heart.[2]

Tocqueville is certainly correct when he suggests that democracy causes individuals to turn their backs on the past. Americans have

2. Alexis de Tocqueville, *Democracy in America*, vol. 2 (New York: Vintage Books, 1990), 99.

always seen themselves as innovators. Thomas Paine, writing in the midst of the American Revolution, famously told American colonists, "We have it in our power to begin the world over again." Sadly, most people have no use for the past. The United States has always been a nation that has looked forward rather than backward. In some respects, American history is the story of the relentless efforts of ordinary Americans to break away from the tyranny of the past. Walt Whitman summed it up best in his tribute to American pioneers: "All the past we leave behind, / We debouch upon a newer mightier world, varied world, / Fresh and strong the world we seize, world of labor and the march, / Pioneers! O Pioneers!"[3]

I regularly encounter college students who ask me why they are required to take a history course when it will probably have no direct bearing on their postgraduation job prospects. And, in most cases, they are right; I have yet to meet a graduate who landed a job because a potential employer was impressed with a grade in History 141. For many the past is foreign and irrelevant. We treat the past as if it is a form of tyranny, something that holds us back.

But Tocqueville is only partially correct. Americans *will* look to the past if they can find something in it that contributes to their pursuits of happiness. Perhaps this explains why we will always find history books near or at the top of the *New York Times* best-seller list. Those who enjoy reading and studying history tend to be a vibrant bunch. As democratic citizens in a capitalist culture committed to progress, Americans seldom reject something— even if it is the past—that gets them where they want to go. If the examination of the past can meet our needs, we Americans will consume it. Indeed, as historian David Thelen has noted, "Using the past is as eating or breathing. It is a common human activity. What we have in common as human beings is that we employ the past to make sense of the present and to influence the future."[4]

3. Walt Whitman, *Leaves of Grass: The Poems of Walt Whitman* (London: Walter Scott, 1886).
4. Roy Rosenzweig and David Thelen, *The Presence of the Past: Popular Uses of History in American Life* (New York: Columbia University Press, 1998), 190.

The "Presence of the Past"

I argued in the previous chapter that history is a discipline that requires interpretation, imagination, and even literary or artistic style. But this is not the way most people perceive the discipline. When I tell people what I do for a living, I often get blank stares. They probably think that as a history professor I earn my keep inflicting undergraduates with an endless barrage of names and dates before forcing them to spew this information back to me on an exam. (Ben Stein's character from *Ferris Bueller's Day Off* again comes to mind.) I blame their reaction on the way history is sometimes taught in schools. Based on a survey of over 1,400 American adults, historian Ron Rosenzweig and Thelen found that people have a strongly negative reaction to the way that history was presented to them. Nearly three-fifths of those surveyed used words such as "irrelevant," "incomplete," "dry," and "boring" to describe their high school history classes.[5]

But Rosenzweig and Thelen also found overwhelming evidence to suggest that Americans regularly and voluntarily engaged in what they call "past related activities." If you think about it, Americans are actually obsessed with the past. They watch the History Channel and historical films, buy history-themed books and novels, make scrapbooks to preserve cherished memories, attend high school reunions, participate in battle reenactments, interview their elders, construct family genealogies, play history-related video games, and preserve old houses. Americans spend their vacations—the precious time in which they get a break from work—visiting places like the Alamo, Gettysburg, Williamsburg, and Philadelphia. Consider the irony. Americans spend millions of dollars each year to explore a subject that many of them hated in school.

Why is there such a palpable "presence of the past," as Rosenzweig and Thelen describe it?[6] We are drawn to engaging with the past for a variety of reasons. In the remainder of this chapter, we will look at a number of these reasons: the past inspires us, the

5. Ibid., 31, 109, 111.
6. Ibid., 9, 18, 19.

past helps us escape the pressures of modern life, the past gives us a sense of self, the past contains people like us, the past helps us envision a better future, and the past enables us to promote our political and social commitments. The past must be relevant. It must be usable. Or at the very least, it cannot be useless.[7]

The Inspirational Past

One way that we use the past is as a source of inspiration. We are moved by the heroism of American soldiers charging onto the beaches of Normandy on June 6, 1944. We admire the moral persistence of William Wilberforce, the nineteenth-century British politician who ended the slave trade in England, or the courage of Nelson Mandela, the South African activist who helped to bring an end to apartheid. Perhaps some of you wrote a celebratory paper in elementary school or high school about George Washington, Susan B. Anthony, Harriet Tubman, Abraham Lincoln, Martin Luther King Jr., Mohandas Gandhi, Lewis and Clark, or Eleanor Roosevelt. Maybe your hero is your great-grandfather who migrated to the United States from an oppressed country and made a better life for himself and his family, or a grandmother who struggled through the Great Depression. Perhaps you have an inspirational quote or two on your desk that was uttered by a figure from the past. The past has the power to stimulate us, fill us with emotion, and arouse our deepest convictions about what is good and right. When we study inspirational figures of the past, we often connect with them through time and leave the encounter wanting to be better people or perhaps even continue their legacy of reform, justice, patriotism, or heroism.

I will never forget Christine—a student who, about eight years ago, took my introductory course in United States history. One of

7. Jane Kamensky, "Fighting (Over) Words: Speech, Power, and the Moral Imagination in American History," in *In the Face of the Facts: Moral Inquiry in American Scholarship*, ed. Richard Wightman Fox and Robert B. Westbrook (Cambridge: Cambridge University Press), 115–16.

the assigned readings in this course was *Common Sense*, Thomas Paine's plea for the American colonies to rebel against England and start a new nation. Paine is an engaging writer—even to first year college students who are not interested in history. As one of the more radical thinkers of his day, Paine not only called for American independence but urged Americans to establish a democratic form of government at a time when many of the founding fathers had serious doubts about whether the "people" could really be trusted to make decisions for the good of the nation. Eighteenth-century society was not yet ready for Paine. He was ahead of his time.

Christine was moved by Paine's passionate pleas for justice. She was attracted to his proposal to give ordinary people (including women and slaves) a role in government. But as an art major, Christine was disappointed with the portrait of Paine on the cover of the edition of *Common Sense* that I had assigned for class. It was a fairly typical portrait of an eighteenth-century figure—staid, sober, and formal. Christine noticed right away that the rather conservative portrait was out of sync with the radical and controversial nature of Paine's ideas. As part of her senior art project, she set out to correct this. By the end of the semester, Christine had produced a new cover for *Common Sense*. It included the original portrait of Paine splashed with fluorescent greens and oranges. The words "Common Sense" were superimposed in the background, and the word "sense" was printed in reverse and upside down. Now this was the Paine whose words had inspired Christine. Such inspiration prompted her to devote her most important piece of college art to this eighteenth-century revolutionary. When my wife heard about Christine's painting, she bought a copy of her work, framed it, and gave it to me for Christmas. Today it hangs in my office and has become a conversation piece about how the past can inspire.

Christians have made good use of this benefit of studying history. Our lives are enriched by learning about great leaders of the Christian faith—St. Francis of Assisi, Thomas Aquinas, Joan of Arc, Martin Luther, John Calvin, Dietrich Bonhoeffer, Jonathan Edwards, William Wilberforce, Emma Willard, Dorothy Day, Mother Teresa, John Paul II, Billy Graham. We are inspired by these figures because we believe that God has used them. By learning their stories, we gain insight into how to live faithfully. Recently I read Thomas Slaughter's wonderful biography of John Woolman, the eighteenth-century Quaker reformer and abolitionist. While Slaughter clearly likes Woolman and what he stood for, he does his best to write as a detached historian. He never overtly offers up Woolman as a figure worthy of emulation. But learning about this Quaker's principled stands against slavery and materialism and reading about the compassionate way he dealt with the people he encountered has inspired me to press on in my own vocation as a Christian.[8]

Recently I gave a lecture at a Christian college about the importance to society of the study of the past, and a perceptive student asked me how I thought history might help the church in its role in fulfilling the Great Commission. I can't remember how I answered him that night, but his question came to mind again a few weeks later as I taught an adult Sunday school lesson about the place of religion in the history of the founding of America. As a good historian, I tried to explain to the class that it is very difficult to generalize about the religious beliefs of the founding fathers or the role of religion in the American Revolution because history is complex and complicated. But I think the class really wanted to hear about Christian heroes of the American Revolution—people motivated by faith who made a difference in forging the birth of the United States. "The Christian church today needs a history lesson." That is what I should have said to that Christian college student. The church needs to be inspired by the way people have fearlessly, through the Holy Spirit's leading, proclaimed and lived the gospel. When was the last time your Christian education director or Sunday school superintendent offered a course in church history? Such a series of lessons might be useful for the way it can inspire the congregation to fulfill its mission.[9]

The past, of course, is also useful as a cautionary tale. It is filled with people who we do not want to emulate. Nero, Attila the Hun,

---

8. Thomas Slaughter, *The Beautiful Soul of John Woolman* (New York: Hill and Wang, 2008).

9. For a further discussion of history's role in the church, see the epilogue.

Pol Pot, Adolf Hitler, Joseph Stalin, Saddam Hussein, and Osama bin Laden come immediately to mind. Sometimes a reflection on the past reveals wrong turns we humans have taken. The history of slavery and segregation in the United States, and the subsequent civil rights movement, should remind us to always judge humans not by the color of their skin but by the content of their character. By exploring the history of our own families, we can see where decisions were made that resulted in brokenness, divorce, abuse, or dysfunction. Sometimes we do not want to follow in the footsteps of our ancestors. The past both inspires us and keeps us out of trouble. George Santayana was correct when he said, "Those who cannot remember the past are condemned to repeat it." Whether it is inspiration or warning, we can all draw lessons for the present by studying the past.

Escape into the Past

For others, the past is useful because it provides an escape from the pressures and anxieties of modern life. One of my favorite episodes of the 1960s television show *The Twilight Zone* is titled "A Stop at Willoughby." The episode features a stressed-out New York advertising executive, named Gart Williams, who is growing tired of the corporate rat race and an overbearing wife who only married him for his ability to provide her with a comfortable upper-middle-class life in the suburbs. One day on his train commute from New York City to his home in Connecticut, Gart falls asleep and dreams that the train, which has turned into a late nineteenth-century rail coach, has stopped at a place called "Willoughby," and the year is 1888. The conductor tells him that Willoughby is a "peaceful, restful place, where a man can slow down to a walk and live his life full measure." Gart glances out the train window and sees a small town with an old-fashioned bandstand, high-wheeler bikes, horse-drawn carriages, and couples strolling through the park. He eventually wakes from his dream, but he becomes fascinated by this town that his imagination created. The following week Gart dreams again about Willoughby and tells himself that the next time the train stops at this fictional town, he is going to get off and leave his old life behind. After another stressful day at work, which leads to a mental breakdown, Gart quits his job and boards his train back to Connecticut. He dozes off again and starts to dream about his late nineteenth-century paradise. This time he gets off the train at Willoughby, where he is greeted by the town's friendly residents who invite him to join them in their idyllic life. At this point, fitting the eerie nature of *The Twilight Zone*, the scene shifts back to a modern-day train conductor standing in the snow over Gart's lifeless body. He tells the police that Gart shouted "something about Willoughby" as he leaped from the moving train to his death.

"A Stop at Willoughby" is a popular episode because we can all relate to the plight of Gart Williams. We all long for a world that has been lost—a haven where we can escape the pressures of daily life. The past, or at least the re-creation or reenactment of the past, can provide such a haven. One website describing Colonial Williamsburg encourages potential visitors to "escape to the 18th century in the world's largest living-history museum."[10] Renaissance Faires attract thousands of visitors each summer, where attendees wear period clothing and come back each weekend to immerse themselves in a different time. Other people prefer to visit a historical site or read historical fiction or nonfiction books as a kind of time travel to a world that was simpler. These kinds of nostalgic longings fuel a billion-dollar historical tourism industry. As David Lowenthal writes,

> The past offers alternatives to an unacceptable present. In yesterday we find what we miss today. And yesterday is a time for which we have no responsibility and when no one can answer back. Some prefer to live permanently in the past; others elect to visit it only occasionally. Even if today is rewarding and the past no golden age, historical immersion can alleviate contemporary stress.[11]

10. "Williamsburg and Hampton Roads Features," Fodor's Travel Intelligence, www.fodors.com/world/north-america/usa/virginia/williamsburg-and-hampton -roads/feature_30001.html.

11. David Lowenthal, *The Past Is a Foreign Country* (New York: Cambridge University Press, 1985), 49–50.

For some, the practice of getting lost in the past is a great form of therapy.

The Past Reminds Us Who We Are

When I ask students why it is important to study history, many of them say that without understanding where we came from, we cannot know who we are. As Lowenthal puts it, "The sureness of 'I was' is a necessary component of the sureness of 'I am.'"[12] The individual obsession over where we came from and who we are is evident in the popular quest to discover our roots. Historical societies, genealogical libraries, and other repositories of public records are often filled with people, usually crouched over microfilm readers, trying to add branches to their family trees. Television programs such as *Who Do You Think You Are?* or Henry Louis Gates's *Finding Your Roots* combine Americans' love of celebrity culture with their desire to know the details of their personal past. In one episode of *Finding Your Roots*, Gates, the director of the W. E. B. Du Bois Institute for African and African American Research at Harvard University and an African American himself, has his own DNA analyzed and is forced to come to grips with the fact that fifty percent of his genetic heritage is European (and that he is actually from the same ancestral tree as talk-show host Regis Philbin). The 1970s television miniseries *Roots* inspired a revival in genealogical research, especially among African Americans. Rosenzweig and Thelen's survey measuring the historical sensibility of ordinary Americans found that most people thought history was important as a means of exploring "where their families had come from and how they had become the kinds of people they were."[13] Many Americans believe that they must turn to the past as a way of facing the future.

The past can also help us understand our place in the communities and nations we call home. McClay writes,

12. Ibid., 41.
13. Rosenzweig and Thelen, *Presence of the Past*, 45–46.

In the end, communities and nation-states are constituted and sustained by such shared memories—by stories of foundation, conflict, and perseverance. The leap of imagination and faith, from the thinness and unreliability of our individual memory to the richness of collective memory, that is the leap of civilized life; and the discipline of collective memory is the task not only of the historian, but of every one of us.[14]

Local, county, and state historical societies, many of them underfunded and understaffed, take their mission to keep the past alive very seriously. I have seen many of their efforts firsthand. For example, in the tiny southern New Jersey town of Greenwich, where I have taken trips with apprentice historians for the purpose of telling the story of a community that is more than three hundred years old, the county historical society conducts regular celebrations of the "Greenwich Tea Burning," a 1774 event in which local patriots burned a shipment of East India tea in response to the Tea Act imposed on the colonies by the British. These celebrations often include historical lectures, residents dressed in period clothing, a reenactment of the tea burning, and a parade down the town's main thoroughfare—Ye Great Street. As my students and I have learned, there is much about the Greenwich Tea Burning celebrations that rests on shaky historical ground. For example, there is no evidence that any of the names on the monument honoring the tea burners in the center of town actually participated in the event. (And, in fact, there were at least two individuals who we can be relatively certain *did* participate in the event whose names are not engraved on the monument.) Tales of secret meeting places, colonists dressed as Indians, and traitors to the cause who tried to take the tea for their own consumption are probably more the product of late nineteenth-century and twentieth-century additions to the story than an accurate portrayal of what actually happened. But despite these historical problems, the Greenwich Tea Burning,

14. Wilfred M. McClay, "The Mystic Chords of Memory," *The Heritage Foundation*, December 13, 1995, www.heritage.org/research/lecture/the-mystic -chords-of-memory-reclaiming-american-history.

and its regular celebration, still serves as a way that the people of this community, many of whom can trace their family trees back to the original settlers, make sense of who they are.

History, of course, also plays a vital part in the forging of a national identity. As soon as the United States was founded, historians began writing about the meaning of the American Revolution in an attempt to remind Americans of the values and ideals for which it was waged. David Ramsey, the author of *History of the American Revolution* (1789), described the events of the Revolutionary War through the grid of divine providence. Mercy Otis Warren, in *History of the Rise, Progress and Termination of the American Revolution* (1805), celebrated the overthrow of English dominion by a small band of colonial soldiers who then created a government based on freedom. Writing in the early nineteenth century, George Bancroft, the author of the multivolume *History of the United States, from Discovery of the American Continent* (1834–74), portrayed the American Revolution as the event that established the United States as a Christian nation created to spread liberty and democracy to the world.[15] We need the stories of our past to sustain us as a people. History is the glue that holds communities and nations together. This is the case not only in the United States but in nearly all modern nation-states. History writing was an important tool in the nineteenth-century transformation of Germany from a collection of provinces into a unified nation. The Department of Canadian Heritage teaches Canadians to learn about their history because it believes history to be a "collective treasure, given to us and ours to bequeath to our children."[16]

In the United States, history has always been used to teach children lessons in patriotism. In the past, history teachers and the writers of history curriculum were careful not to portray the country in

15. Peter Messer, *Stories of Independence: Identity, Ideology, and History in Eighteenth-Century America* (DeKalb: Northern Illinois Press, 2005); John Fea, *Was America Founded as a Christian Nation? A Historical Introduction* (Louisville: Westminster John Knox, 2011), 9.

16. John Tosh, introduction to *Historians on History*, ed. John Tosh (Essex, UK: Pearson Education, 2000), 6; Margaret MacMillan, *Dangerous Games: The Uses and Abuses of History* (New York: Modern Library, 2009), 4.

a negative light. Duke University historian W. T. Laprade, writing in 1934, described the purpose of teaching history in schools as "the inculcation of a species of patriotic religion."[17] Lucy Salmon, a historian who served on a committee of the American Historical Association devoted to the teaching of history in public schools, wanted schools to teach heroism in their American history courses. The curriculum, she argued, must avoid "the presentation to children of . . . blemishes the world has gladly forgiven and forgotten for the sake of a great work accomplished and a noble life lived."[18] In the early twentieth century, patriotic organizations railed on Harvard history professor Albert Bushnell Hart for telling his students that during the Stamp Act crisis of 1765, "the colonists liked to think of themselves as part of the British empire . . . [and] were proud of being Britons." Though such an assertion was true, Hart was accused of treason and pro-British propaganda.[19]

The civic nature of public-school history education has been a source of great controversy in recent years. In 1994 conservatives challenged the proposed "National History Standards" because they supposedly gave too much space to minorities, women, and ordinary people and not enough space to the founding fathers, the Constitution, and other white males. Gary Nash, one of the authors of the national standards, described the controversy as "an expression of a country's historical image of itself and the intertwining of public memory with national purpose."[20] Around the same time, the school board of Lake County, Florida, required that students learn that American culture and values are "superior to other foreign or historic cultures." Opponents called the requirement "jingoistic," affirming that American culture is made up of

17. W. T. Laprade, "The Function of the Historian," *Social Studies* 25 (1934): 74, quoted in Peter Novick, *That Noble Dream: The "Objectivity Question" and the American Historical Profession* (New York: Cambridge University Press, 1988), 246.

18. Lucy Salmon, "Some Principles in the Teaching of History," National Society for the Scientific Study of Education, *Yearbook* 1 (1902): 51, quoted in Novick, *That Noble Dream*, 71.

19. Gary Nash, *History on Trial: Culture Wars and the Teaching of the Past* (New York: Vintage, 2000), 29.

20. Ibid., xvi.

many different cultures from around the world and, as a result, those cultures must be studied for their contribution to United States history.[21] And, most recently, the conservatives in control of the Texas Board of Education rewrote the state's history standards to remove what they perceived to be the undue influence of multicultural revisionism and the failure to incorporate Judeo-Christian values into the curriculum.[22]

The battle over what American schoolchildren learn about the nation's past has been a significant part of the ongoing culture wars in this country. But even when historians write in a fashion that criticizes national ambition or chides the nation for its past sins, such writing can serve a civic purpose. In the United States, liberal or progressive historians—who, for example, call attention to the slaveholding of the founding fathers, or to the failure of the United States to apply the principles of democracy to all, or to the dark side of American imperialism—often write with a sense that a complete picture of the American past, warts and all, is useful in the creation of thoughtful citizens and critical thinkers. History textbook authors who refuse to sugarcoat the past are being just as patriotic as those who believe public-school education should instill students with a reverence for the United States and its past. When historians report the truth—whether the news is good or bad—they are doing their jobs well. As historian Walter McDougall writes, "The civic purpose of history cannot be abolished, since all history—traditional or subversive of tradition—has a civic effect."[23]

The attempts to use the past to promote a particular understanding of politics, religion, national identity, or some other present-day cause, risk replacing "history" with "heritage." "Heritage" is a term that historians do not like very much. The purpose of heritage,

21. Quoted in Kamensky, "Fighting (Over) Words," 144; Larry Rohter, "Battle of Patriotism Curriculum," *New York Times*, May 15, 1994, http://hettingern.people .cofc.edu/Intro_to_Philosophy_Sp_06/Superior_Culture_Policy.htm.
22. For a thorough discussion of the Texas standards controversy, see "TEKS Watch," a website associated with the University of Texas–El Paso, http://organiza tions.utep.edu/Default.aspx?tabid=65763.
23. Walter McDougall, Special Symposium on "Teaching American History," *The American Scholar* (Winter 1998): 101.

writes Lowenthal, is to "domesticate the past" so that it can be enlisted "for present causes." (We will examine this practice more fully in the next chapter.) It is a way of approaching the past that is fundamentally different than the discipline of history. History explores and explains the past in all its fullness and complexity. Heritage calls attention to the past to make a political point; it is rarely concerned with nuance or paradox. Lowenthal describes the devotion to heritage as something akin to a spiritual calling. It is intricately wed to civil religion and nationalism. Heritage crusades often emerge during times of societal change and progress. "Beleaguered by loss and change," Lowenthal writes, "we keep our bearings only by clinging to remnants of stability." For example, the people of Greenwich, New Jersey, have called on their sense of themselves as residents of a seventeenth-century village as a way of navigating a host of changes to their rural community, including the rise of industrialization and the influx of new immigrants into the southern New Jersey countryside. This past provides a sense of comfort and security to the residents of the town through its appeal to what they believe to be a simpler time. On a national level, we engage in heritage crusades when we promote mythical or celebratory views of the past—such as the story of George Washington chopping down the cherry tree or the triumphant settling of the West—that give us a feel-good sense of collective identity.[24]

Christians also turn to the past in search of identity. Christianity, of course, is a historic religion. Christians rest their faith on a historic event—the life, death, burial, and resurrection of Jesus Christ. We find guidance and spiritual authority in church tradition and the teachings of a divinely inspired book—the Bible. Some branches of Christianity, particularly Roman Catholicism and Eastern Orthodoxy, believe that the tradition of the church is a living tradition. The men and women of faith who have gone before us, who have articulated most clearly the teachings of the church, not only inspire us (as we discussed above) but provide us

24. David Lowenthal, *The Heritage Crusade and the Spoils of History* (Cambridge: Cambridge University Press, 1998), xv, 1–3, 6.

with theological guideposts that help us live our faith and define the boundaries of our faith in an ever-changing world. Even Protestants, who largely reject the divine authority of church tradition, still cling to holy books that were assembled into our current Old and New Testaments by Christians who were the products of a particular time and place. This sacred and historical book is essential to forging our identities as modern-day Christians. When we stop following the teachings of the Bible, we can no longer claim an identity as Christians.

History is also useful for Christians in helping us to forge religious identities among different traditions in the history of the church. Many evangelicals, for example, have been critical of their tradition for its failure to engage the rich history of Christendom. Some of these evangelicals have challenged their fellow believers to read the writings of the early church fathers in hopes that exposure to these saints will result in a richer and more rooted faith. Others have abandoned evangelicalism completely, finding homes in Anglicanism, Catholicism, or Eastern Orthodoxy—traditions that seek a more ancient faith, one that is connected in a deeper way to the past. In my own life, I have moved in an opposite direction from those described above. As a teenage convert to evangelicalism, I have found that the history of American evangelicalism—a subfield of American religious history that was coming of age as I entered adulthood and began to contemplate a life in the historical profession—helped me make sense of my new identity as an evangelical Christian. By turning to the past, and specifically to the work of historians such as Mark Noll, George Marsden, Nathan Hatch, and Randall Balmer, I have been able to make sense of the strange (from the perspective of my childhood Catholicism) evangelical subculture I had joined when I was sixteen years old. History served as a valuable guide on my youthful religious journey. It continues to be useful in helping me to make sense of my religious identity today.

I recently finished teaching a course titled "Early American Republic," which focused on the twenty-five years of American history following the ratification of the Constitution. One of the books that I assigned in this course was Nathan Hatch's *The Democratization of American Christianity*.[25] The rationale for assigning this text was to get students—many of them evangelical Christians—to see the powerful grip that evangelicalism held over American culture during this period. By reading Hatch, my students learned that early nineteenth-century evangelicalism was successful because it relied on emotional preaching that appealed more to the passions than to reason, it rejected tradition in an attempt to return to the teachings of the New Testament church, it challenged Calvinist doctrines that placed limits on the ability of humans to participate in their own salvation, it utilized the most current forms of communication to spread its message, it exchanged traditional singing for folk music (do I hear praise songs?), it embraced a theology informed more by common sense than by learned theological discourse, it was driven by the needs and wants of the people in the pews (religious consumerism), and it was associated with charismatic leaders who could appeal to the masses. After a thorough reading of *The Democratization of American Christianity*, I asked my students if any of this sounded familiar. Most of them recognized these characteristic traits of American evangelicalism from their churches and their religious upbringings. Hatch's book offers insight into a movement in the past that was familiar to them. My students learned an important lesson about the continuity between the past and the present, and they came away with a deeper understanding of the religious communities in which they were raised.

The Past as Familiar

When we think about the way the past might be relevant or useful in our lives, familiarity is also important. We tend to search the past for people like us. As Margaret MacMillan notes, "When people talk, as they frequently do, about the need for 'proper' history, what they

25. Nathan O. Hatch, *The Democratization of American Christianity* (New Haven: Yale University Press, 1991).

really mean is the history they want and like."[26] We want to learn about those in the past who felt the way we feel, who endured the same trials and tribulations that we endure, and who experienced the same joys and triumphs that we experience. Though societies change over time, there is much about the human experience—birth, death, suffering, sex, fear, work, joy—that does not.

One of the reasons schoolchildren find history to be boring or dry is that they cannot relate to the universal or national narratives of the past that they find in their textbooks. Rosenzweig and Thelen have found that people become more engaged with the past when they can make personal connections with historical figures with whom they can relate.[27] This is why history, and particularly history education, has become embroiled of late in the culture wars. In response to the concern that students are not finding people like them in their school curriculum, districts have made a conscious effort to season their textbooks and standards with multicultural voices, the voices of the poor and lower classes, and the voices of women. The hope is that students of color, students in poverty, and female students will feel more at home in the history classroom when they encounter familiar historical actors. In colleges and universities, specialized programs in African American studies, gender studies, Native American studies, queer studies, and social history have been trying to meet the need for this kind of usable past for a long time. Critics of this kind of multicultural history argue that students should be learning a national narrative that introduces them to a common set of values, ideals, and historical actors that all Americans can embrace. These kinds of debates illustrate the ever-present desire for a usable past.

The Progressive Vision of the Past

For twentieth-century historians described as "progressives" or "neoprogressives," the past was useful as a means of promoting

26. MacMillan, *Dangerous Games*, 113.
27. Rosenzweig and Thelen, *Presence of the Past*, 111–13, 133.

social reform. The turn-of-the-century historian Carl Becker announced that "historical thinking is a social instrument, helping in getting the world's work more effectively done." He called his fellow historians to "exploit" the past in order to advance necessary social reforms.[28] During World War I, it was not uncommon for professional historians to participate in the production of war propaganda. Since the war had a progressive purpose—to spread democracy abroad—historians saw their participation in the war effort as a means of promoting their political and ideological views. Historian James Harvey Robinson had to make multiple revisions to a history textbook he was writing because his editors deemed its contents not to be sufficiently anti-German.[29]

The progressive view of history reached new heights during the 1950s and 1960s as young historians became involved in the major social issues of the day. As these historians began to speak out against the injustices that they saw in society, they began to articulate a method of approaching the past that was concerned less with objectivity and more with activism. They looked to the past for antecedents to contemporary social problems that might help point the world in the right direction.[30] These historians, to various degrees, made their political convictions known. Some of them had roots in the Communist Party and others were connected to the so-called New Left, a growing group of activists shaped by their Marxism, campus protests, fight for civil rights, and opposition to America's involvement in Vietnam. They wrote books calling attention to the nation's long history of injustice. Such works were largely one-sided, but that was the point. Textbooks, they believed, were too slanted toward the so-called establishment, which they believed to be dominated by elite white male politicians, corporate interests, plantation owners, and warmongers. Their vocation was to focus on the human experience from the perspective of the poor,

28. Carl Becker, "Some Aspects of the Influence of Social Problems and Ideas upon the Study and Writing of History," *American Journal of Sociology* 18 (1912–1913): 663, quoted in Novick, *That Noble Dream*, 98.

29. Novick, *That Noble Dream*, 116–18, 128.

30. Ibid., 350–51, 354.

impoverished, and dispossessed. Howard Zinn, one of the most popular of these writers, had a very clear view of what historians should be doing in the midst of these tumultuous times:

> If we start from the ethical assumption that it is fundamentally wrong to hold in bondage . . . another human being, and that the freeing of such persons requires penetrating the moral sensibilities of a nation, then it is justifiable to focus on those aspects of the complexity which support this goal. . . . You are not telling the whole truth . . . but you are emphasizing that portion of the truth which supports a morally desirable action.[31]

Progressive historians also led the way in replacing the study of history in schools with the study of what they came to call "social studies," an approach that emphasized the "social efficiency" of education. History would be part of the larger umbrella of "social studies" as long as it could be related to the present needs of students. Rather than memorizing names, dates, and obscure information about Mesopotamia or European explorers, progressive reformers believed that students should spend more time applying the lessons of history to real-life events. History needed to be useful. Charles Beard, the leading progressive historian whom we met in the previous chapter, was a strong supporter of replacing history with social studies because, as he put it, "History which does not emerge into the living present is sterile when viewed from the standpoint of public need." Becker thought that economics and government should share space in the school curriculum with history. The vision of these progressives continues to hold sway in our schools today. History must serve present needs or else it is useless and not particularly worthy of study by children.[32]

31. Howard Zinn, "Abolitionists, Freedom-Riders, and the Tactics of Agitation," in *The Antislavery Vanguard: New Essays on the Abolitionists*, ed. Martin Duberman (Princeton: Princeton University Press, 1965), quoted in Novick, *That Noble Dream*, 431. These neoprogressives included Zinn, Staughton Lynd, Jesse Lemisch, and, to a certain extent, Eugene Genovese, Herbert Gutman, and Christopher Lasch.
32. Ibid., 188–89.

Summing Up

The past is everywhere. Take some time to think about the many ways you encountered the past today. Perhaps you shared a memory with a family member or looked at some old photos on Facebook. Or maybe you spent some time thinking about how the past has shaped who you are today. The past serves our needs in a variety of ways. We consume the past in hopes that it will inspire us, provide an escape from modern life, and tell us who we are as individuals and communities. We enter the past in search of people like us, and we invoke the past in our political and cultural debates. We cannot escape its presence in our lives. So why not embrace it? As we will see in the next chapter, attempts at making the past relevant must be done with caution, but we should not be shy about linking the past to the present. If you are a historian, part of your responsibility is to inform the general public about the way the past connects to our contemporary lives and to help the members of your community use the past to make meaning of their lives. As those living in the "here and now," we are in constant dialogue with the past, whether we realize it or not. As long as we remain products of an American culture that celebrates the individual and his or her quest to bring order to life, we will live in a paradoxical relationship to what has come before us. The past will always serve as a temper to the progressive vision of a better world, but we will appeal to it endlessly in order to make that world a reality.

3

The Past Is a Foreign Country

THE HISTORIAN DAVID LOWENTHAL TELLS THE STORY OF a Midwestern man's visit to Plimoth Plantation, the living history museum in Plymouth, Massachusetts, that interprets the earliest days of the seventeenth-century settlement of New England. Lowenthal witnessed this man—this "booster of individualism and free enterprise"—have an interesting encounter with the actor playing William Bradford, the governor of Plymouth Colony. Lowenthal writes,

> Like many Americans, this visitor grew up in the faith that the Pilgrim Fathers were true begetters of his own values. Now he was finding *this* prototype Father's views diametrically opposed to his own. Bradford was a Calvinist predestinarian, a believer in community to whom secular capitalist enterprise was blasphemous, selfish individualism anathema. Seething with indignation, the visitor could not just dismiss pious Bradford as a crank or a Communist. . . . For the first time in his life, this visitor confronted a world view fundamentally at odds with his own and had to engage with it as an idea.[1]

1. David Lowenthal, "Dilemmas and Delights of Learning History," in *Knowing, Teaching, and Learning History: National and International Perspectives*, ed.

Indeed, William Bradford lived in a world that was quite different from the world of this Midwestern visitor or, for that matter, anyone born and raised in the modern United States. This man learned an important lesson about trying to superimpose his system of belief on the past. As Lowenthal, echoing the late novelist L. P. Hartley, reminds us, "The past is a foreign country: they do things differently there."[2]

As we saw in the last chapter, we are all in search of a usable past—a past that we can consume or put to good use as we live our lives in the present. But sometimes the past is not easily consumable. Sometimes what happened in previous eras has no direct relevance for our lives today. It is this seeming irrelevance of the past that turns off many to its study. What if the past does not inspire us or help us to understand ourselves? What if we are required to investigate an era or a movement that, at first glance, does not seem to teach us anything about our society? How does knowledge of the medieval feudal system help us live better lives? Will our lives be enriched by a thorough understanding of the causes of World War I?

Similarly, the past often forces us to confront characters or events that seem utterly strange to us. People in the past burned witches. People engaged in human sacrifice. Some people, as this Midwestern man found out, were not free-market capitalists. We often find that our feeble attempts at making the past usable run headlong into the words and ideas of people of the past. In the last chapter, we covered the "presence of the past." In this chapter, we explore the "pastness of the past." We will come to grips with the reality that what happened long ago, in all its strangeness and foreignness, may not always be as usable as we would like it to be. While the last chapter examined the continuities that exist between the past and the present, in this chapter we focus on the discontinuities, or the inherent "otherness," of the past.[3]

Peter N. Stearns, Peter Seixas, and Sam Wineburg (New York: New York University Press, 2000), 74–75.

2. David Lowenthal, *The Past Is a Foreign Country* (New York: Cambridge University Press, 1999) and L. P. Hartley, *The Go-Between* (New York: New York Review Book, 1953), 17.

3. On the "pastness of the past," see Gordon S. Wood, *The Purpose of the Past: Reflections on the Uses of History* (New York: Penguin, 2008), 9.

Historicism

One of the most important critics of a usable past was the nineteenth-century German historian Leopold von Ranke (1795–1886). He introduced the concept of "historicism," or the idea that historians should seek to understand the past on its own terms. Historicism has since become a mainstay of the historical profession. As Ranke put it, "History has had assigned to it the task of judging the past, or instructing the present for the benefit of ages to come. To such lofty functions this work does not aspire. Its aim is to know how things happened."[4] Ranke wanted historians to study the past for its own sake, not because it has a usable function for guiding our lives in the present. He rejected the notion that the past is useful in that it teaches moral lessons, inspires those who study it, strengthens civic bonds, or provides individuals and communities with a better sense of identity. Rather, for him, history is a science, and historians can reach the Enlightenment ideal of objectivity in their work. The task of the historian is a conservative one—to seek after objective truth and to narrate "what happened" in the past. No more and no less.[5]

Other historians followed suit. In 1931 English historian Herbert Butterfield (1900–1979) published *The Whig Interpretation of History*. In this oft-cited work, Butterfield criticizes those historians who constructed narratives of the past with the intention of glorifying the present. The goal of the English Whig historians, Butterfield argues, was to tell a story of society's inevitable progression toward liberty. Such an approach would lead the historian to focus only on those aspects of the past that contributed to enlightened or democratic ends. "Whig" history, a phrase coined by Butterfield, was drawn from the British Whig Party, whose members advocated the power of Parliament over and against the members of the Tory Party, the supporters of the king.[6] Whig history has also played a

4. Quoted in Julian J. Gwyn, "Moral Judgments in History," *Revue de l'Universite' d' Ottawa* 34 (1964): 222.
5. John Tosh, *The Pursuit of History*, 3rd ed. (New York: Longman, 2002), 6–8.
6. Herbert Butterfield, *The Whig Interpretation of History* (repr.; New York: W. W. Norton, 1965).

dominant role in American historiography, particularly in the field of early American history. Until recently, much of colonial American history was interpreted as setting the stage for the American Revolution. In other words, pre-Revolutionary history had a certain *telos*—the forward progression to American freedom as embodied in the Declaration of Independence. The purpose of studying colonial history was not to gain a better understanding of life in this era for its own sake, or to explore the British, French, or Spanish influence on the colonies. Rather, the colonies were important because they were the starting point for a narrative that ultimately ended with the Revolution and the emergence of American democracy—a narrative that glorified the present, thus making it useful to society.

As the twentieth century progressed, historicism took new forms. One of the most influential movements to find its anchor in historicism was the so-called Cambridge School. Its most prominent proponent, Quentin Skinner (1940–), demanded that the past always be studied in context. The historians of the Cambridge School turned their attention to intellectual and political history, particularly ideas as embodied in what today we might call "great texts." As extreme contextualists, these historians argued that ideas must always be understood in light of the time period in which they were written. This led the members of the Cambridge School to affirm that authors such as Augustine, Machiavelli, Thomas Hobbes, and others could not offer timeless truths that transcended eras and generations. Instead, these classic writers were products of their time and thus must be understood as such. They could not speak to the concerns— whether they be moral or political—of those living in future eras.[7]

Similarly, the French Annales School was deeply committed to a form of Rankean historicism. The Annales School was named after *Annales d'histoire economique et sociale* (*Annals of Economic and Social History*), a scholarly journal founded and edited by historians Marc Bloch and Lucien Febvre in 1929. The historians of the Annales movement were committed to an interdisciplinary

---

7. Stephanie Lawson, "Is the Future a Foreign Country?," *Australian Journal of Politics and History* 57 (September 2011): 422–23.

approach to the study of the past. They employed insights from history, anthropology, economics, geography, and sociology and tended to work with traditional documentary sources as well as literature, maps, and folklore. Unlike historians of previous generations, and many of their own generation, Annales historians turned their attention away from traditional subjects like politics, war, and biography and instead produced what has been called "big history." This kind of "big history" tends to focus on collective mindsets and long-term change over time.

The Annales movement rejected certain dimensions of historicism, especially Ranke's insistence that the historian remain completely objective. The past, they argued, was too distant for historians to be able to chronicle it in a complete and value-free fashion. But the practitioners of the Annales School did draw on historicism in their emphasis on uncovering the cultural consciousness or *mentalite* (mentality) of a particular time. Annales historians became proficient at using insights from anthropology to explain the lost worlds of the past through an examination of the rituals and other cultural practices and assumptions that defined those worlds. The goal was to explain a culture that was very different from our own and elucidate as best as possible why people in other eras—many of whom were ordinary people shaped by larger cultural forces—behaved in the way that they did.[8]

Historicism continues to find a home in the mainstream historical profession. Throughout the twentieth century, American historicists spoke out strongly against the attempts by progressive historians to use the past to make the world a better place. For example, during World War I, as many progressive historians began writing propaganda to show their patriotism, historians wrestled with whether such activity was somehow compromising the historian's commitment to objectivity. Others attacked historians such as Carl Becker and Charles Beard, progressive scholars who both served terms as president of the American Historical Association

---

8. John Arnold, *History: A Very Short Introduction* (New York: Oxford University Press, 2000), 98–105; Norman J. Wilson, *History in Crisis? Recent Directions in Historiography* (Upper Saddle River, NJ: Prentice Hall, 1999), 63–69.

(AHA), for their support of replacing the study of history in schools with social studies. During the 1950s and 1960s, historicists criticized the neoprogressive or "New Left" historians for letting their ideological commitments distort their understanding of the past.[9]

The debate between traditional historicists and progressive historians reached a fever pitch at the 1969 meeting of the AHA. During this particular meeting, historians who had embraced the political convictions of the New Left attempted to get the organization to pass a resolution against the Vietnam War. These radical historians, who included Staughton Lynd, Howard Zinn, Arthur Waskow, and Jesse Lemisch, to name a few, had hoped for the support of Eugene Genovese, a distinguished historian of the American South, one of the nation's foremost Marxist historians, and a leading opponent of the war in Vietnam. As debate raged at the AHA business meeting, Genovese shocked many of his fellow New Left historians when he led the opposition to the resolution. Genovese, speaking as a historian in a national meeting of historians, made clear his belief that a formal statement of opposition to the war in Vietnam would unnecessarily politicize the profession. By calling the New Left historians "totalitarians" and exhorting the AHA membership to "put them down, put them down hard, once and for all," he sent a message about the vocation of the historian. Though Genovese was one of the most politically active academics in the United States, as a historian he rejected "the cynical conclusion that all scholarship is subjective and 'ideological.'" Historical scholars should not use their scholarship to promote political causes.[10]

Genovese was correct. Good scholars of the past must, at some level, practice historicism. By trying to understand the past on its own terms, the historian treats it with integrity rather than manipulating it or superimposing his or her values on it to advance an agenda in the present. Practicing good history in this regard

9. Peter Novick, *That Noble Dream: The "Objectivity Question" and the American Historical Profession* (New York: Cambridge University Press, 1988), 115–16, 118, 270, 354.

10. Ibid., 437; Ronald Radosh, *Commies: A Journey Through the Old Left, the New Left and the Leftover Left* (San Francisco: Encounter Books, 2001), 149–50.

is not easy. Humans tend to be present-minded when it comes to confronting the past. The discipline of history was never meant to function as a means of getting one's political point across or convincing people to join a cause. The words of historian Beverly Southgate sound harsh, but they are true:

> Ideologically committed historians—those who can be seen to use ("abuse") the past for their own purposes—forfeit the very name of historian; bought off by dominant powers, they are nothing less than corrupt, professional turncoats; and they can be readily detected, falsifying national narratives, in less fortunate parts of the world.[11]

Yet, as we saw in chapter 2, Americans use the past for these purposes all the time. Such an approach to the past can easily degenerate into a form of propaganda or, as the historian Bernard Bailyn described it, "indoctrination by historical example."[12]

It is easy to ignore or dismiss the parts of the past that we do not like. Yet all historians must come to grips with its utter strangeness. Too much present-mindedness makes for bad history. As noted historian of the American West Richard White writes,

> Any good history begins in strangeness. The past should not be comfortable. The past should not be a familiar echo of the present, for if it is familiar, why revisit it? The past should be so strange that you wonder how you and people you know and love could come from such a time.[13]

Or consider the words of historian Carlo Ginzburg:

> The historian's task is just the opposite of what most of us were taught to believe. He must destroy our sense of proximity to the people of the past because they come from societies very different

---

11. Beverly Southgate, "'A Pair of White Gloves': Historians and Ethics," *Rethinking History* 10 (March 2006): 53.

12. Quoted in Gordon Wood, "Reading the Founders' Minds," *New York Review of Books* 54 (June 28, 2007).

13. Quoted in Sam Wineburg, *Historical Thinking and Other Unnatural Acts: Charting the Future of Teaching the Past* (Philadelphia: Temple University Press, 2001), 11.

from our own. The more we discover about these people's mental universes, the more we should be shocked by the cultural distance that separates us from them.[14]

Gordon Wood has said that if someone wants to use the study of the past to change the world, he should forgo a career as a historian and run for office.[15] While it is certainly a worthwhile exercise to use the past to critique a particular dimension of contemporary society, historians, by vocation, are not primarily cultural critics. The task of historians is to pursue the truth, wherever it may lead. They work with original or primary documents to reconstruct the past in all its complexity and fullness. While historians might choose the subject they will study based on current events or personal interest, they must always let the evidence speak, even if that evidence leads them toward a conclusion that might not be useful. Historian James Banner has put it best:

> Being concerned with the past, works of history can only imply, they cannot as history propose, courses of action; they can evaluate, sometimes magisterially, the conditions of society and culture, but they cannot as history directly help society out of its predicaments. The historians of greatest weight and influence tell stories of times gone by rather than analyze current affairs. They charge the present with meaning by locating it in the past; they do not, and cannot, convey us into the future. . . . Their work must stand or fall, not on the temperament or ideology their authors bring to it, not on their works' arguments for change, but instead on their foundations in knowledge and the power of their presentation. Reform may arise from historical knowledge, but bringing about reform is the province of others—or at least of historians on their days off.[16]

Historian Stephanie Lawson has described three kinds of present-minded or anachronistic history. First, present-minded historians assume "unwarranted continuities between the past." As we have

14. Ibid., 10.
15. Wood, *Purpose of the Past*, 308.
16. James M. Banner Jr., *Being a Historian: An Introduction to the Professional World of History* (New York: Cambridge University Press, 2012), 164.

seen, there are indeed many ways in which we can see the continuity between the past and the present, but sometimes efforts to connect the past to the present result in strange analogies. For example, I was recently lecturing to a group of well-informed history buffs about Thomas Jefferson and slavery. We were discussing Jefferson's view of race, particularly his comments in his *Notes on the State of Virginia* about the inherent cultural and intellectual inferiority of Africans. During the question-and-answer session after the talk, a woman asked me what Jefferson would have thought about having a United States president of African descent. Her question implied that Jefferson would have strongly opposed Barack Obama because as an African American Obama was not civilized enough to run the country effectively. When I suggested that we would never know how Jefferson might have responded to the prospect of an Obama presidency, the woman seemed surprised. What she failed to understand was that the early American world had a profoundly different understanding of race from what we have today. She wanted to take Jefferson's world and apply it to the twenty-first-century world in which she lived. This is a form of presentism. It is a faulty way of using the past to speak to matters in the present. It implies continuity between past and present that we have no way of knowing exists. To put it another way, it is a failure to apply the historical thinking skill of "change over time."

Second, Lawson notes, practitioners of presentism project their "own values back in to the past in order to pass inappropriate moral judgment." As we will see in chapter 5, it is easy to take our ethical categories and superimpose them on the past, but this is not the primary task of the historian. The historian is after understanding, not judgment. Allow me to illustrate this point from a typical United States history survey course. At an appropriate point in the semester, I give students copies of documents written by nineteenth-century Southerners—theologians and ministers mostly—who defended the institution of slavery. These writings are completely foreign to my students. Many of them are appalled by the way these Southerners used the Bible to justify their "peculiar institution." They immediately want to critique the arguments of these men from the perspective of their own moral or ethical commitments. Many of them will offer insights from their Bible or theology classes as arguments for why these slaveholders misunderstood the teachings of Scripture, despite the fact that the New Testament never directly condemns slavery.

Thinking about the ethical dimensions of nineteenth-century slaveholding can be an intellectually stimulating and morally helpful exercise, but it should not be the primary focus of a history classroom. Historians are after understanding. They must avoid what historian James LaGrand has described as "preaching through history."[17] Before condemning these pro-slavery advocates, history students need to know why someone from the nineteenth century would see the need to make such a defense of slavery. What was the context in which these documents were written? Who was the intended audience? What were the main issues at stake in the author's arguments? It is important that students enter into the world of a slaveholder and make an effort to empathize with him, no matter how repulsed they are by his words. In the end, engaging the past in this way can eventually result in a much more nuanced and rich critique of pro-slavery views.

Finally, Lawson argues that presentism leads to "interpreting the past improperly for the purpose of legitimating something in the present." I have found this historical fallacy to be especially relevant in the debate over the so-called Christian origins of the United States. As I argue in *Was America Founded as a Christian Nation?*, it is very easy to find something useful in the past that serves a particular political agenda. This is the ultimate form of indoctrination by historical example. For example, those who want to prove that the roots of the United States are Christian can find quotes from the founding fathers in which they reference the importance of God or Christianity to the moral health of a successful republic. Similarly, those who want to prove that the roots of the United States are secular in nature can find quotes from

17. James B. LaGrand, "Preaching Through History," in *Confessing History: Christian Faith and the Historian's Vocation*, ed. John Fea, Jay Green, and Eric Miller (Notre Dame, IN: Notre Dame University Press, 2010).

the founders in which they champion religious freedom or deny essential theological doctrines that have always been at the heart of Christian faith. This kind of cherry-picking does little to help us understand the past in all its fullness. Though it might be an effective way of winning political points in our ongoing culture wars, it is simply bad history.[18]

Similarly, the noted early American historian Gordon Wood, in a review published in *The New Republic* in October 2000, criticized the late historian John Patrick Diggins's interpretation of Abraham Lincoln in the latter's book *On Hallowed Ground: Abraham Lincoln and the Foundations of American History*. Wood was scathing in his critique of Diggins's historical methodology. He said that Diggins "is not really a historian" because he fails to "have a historian's feel for the complexity, the nuances, the contexts, and the differentness of the past." He accused Diggins of thinking about history "as a social scientist might think of it: as a source for generalizations about human behavior that transcend time and place." For Wood, real historians do not make "transhistorical generalizations about human behavior" but understand events "as they actually were, in all their peculiar contexts and circumstances." According to Wood, Diggins had used Lincoln's life as a moral lesson for today and did not have any interest in situating Lincoln in his mid-nineteenth-century world.[19]

This kind of presentism is also prevalent in the writings and teachings of historians who focus on one particular social group, usually a group that has (in one way or another) been marginalized in either the course of history or in the prevailing narrative of the way history is told. Such histories are usually driven by themes of oppression or resistance. Unfortunately, too much of this history is guided by the identity politics of the historian. As a result, the overemphasis on themes of injustice or revolution or radicalism leads historians to exclude material that, as John Tosh puts it, "fits

18. Lawson, "Is the Future a Foreign Country?," 423; John Fea, *Was America Founded as a Christian Nation? A Historical Introduction* (Louisville: Westminster John Knox, 2011).
19. Wood, *Purpose of the Past*, 271–76.

less neatly with the political progamme of the writer." Too often these scholars and teachers of the past fail to make any "serious efforts" to "understand the experience of other groups with a part in the story." Such identity politics are particularly dangerous to the teaching of history.[20] Recently, a fellow historian informed me that she wanted her students to "find themselves" in her class. While this is certainly a worthy exercise and an effective way of getting students to connect with the past, it also lets the students off the hook by excusing them from making any effort to understand people from the past who are different.

Empathy and Humility

If the past is indeed a foreign country, how does a historian navigate such a strange place? Any historical investigation of the past requires two important virtues: empathy and humility. Let's explore these virtues further.

As historian John Cairns notes, empathy "is the passport to gaining a genuine entry into the past as a foreign land, and something distinct from our time."[21] Empathy requires the historian to step into the shoes of historical actors in order to see the world as they did, to understand them on their own terms and not ours. Historian John Lewis Gaddis writes, "Getting inside other people's minds requires that your own mind be open to their impressions—their hopes and fears, their beliefs and dreams, their sense of right and wrong, their perception of the world and where they fit within it."[22] The practice of empathy may be the hardest part of being a historian. This is largely because our natural inclination, or, as Sam Wineburg calls it, our "psychological condition at rest," is to find something useful in the past. We want to make the past work for us rather than enter into it with an attitude of wonder about

20. Tosh, *Pursuit of History*, 182.
21. John Cairns, "Some Reflections on Empathy in History," *Teaching History* 55 (April 1989): 17.
22. John Lewis Gaddis, *The Landscape of History: How Historians Map the Past* (New York: Oxford University Press, 2002), 124.

what we might find and the kinds of people and ideas we might encounter. Historical empathy thus requires an act of the imagination. The practice of bracketing our own ways of seeing the world in order to see a strange world more clearly requires discipline on the part of the historian. It demands a certain level of intellectual maturity. It requires a willingness to listen to the past. Historian Rachel Fulton has described it well in the context of her work on medieval devotional practices:

> To take this leap [of empathizing with our subjects], to attempt, however imperfectly, the refiguration in our understanding of the configuration given through narrative of the prefigurative action of the past . . . is neither historiographically presumptive nor critically naïve but quintessentially *human*: it is to acknowledge both ourselves and others as simultaneously agents and sufferers of that past; it is to acknowledge that the writing of history is itself an act of compassion as much as it is an act of participation but also of understanding; moreover, it is a refusal of self as potentially mutable, of the possibility of conversion in the encounter with an Other, for what is conversion if not the willingness to look at the world through another's eyes, to see the lens of another's reality—and to accept it, if only momentarily, as one's own?[23]

Empathy differs from sympathy. Empathy is all about understanding. It is an attempt to discover why a particular individual in the past acted in the way that he or she did. It might even mean exploring such actions in an attempt to grasp how he or she reflects the mentality of all of those living in that time and how such a mentality differs from our own. Sympathy, however, carries a deeper moral component than empathy. The sympathetic person develops an emotional attachment—such as a desire for the other person to be happy—that can sometimes make empathy difficult and might even get in the way of an accurate historical interpretation.[24]

23. Rachel Fulton, *From Judgment to Passion: Devotion to Christ and the Virgin Mary, 800–1200* (New York: Columbia University Press, 2002), 470.
24. Cairns, "Some Reflections," 13–18; Jason L. Endacott, "Reconsidering Affective Engagement in Historical Empathy," *Theory and Research in Social Education* 38:1 (Winter 2010): 11–12.

To illustrate the differences between empathy and sympathy, let me relay a conversation I recently had with my fourteen-year-old daughter. Allyson had just finished reading Harriet A. Jacobs's *Incidents in the Life of a Slave Girl, Written by Herself*, in her eighth-grade American Studies class. Published in 1861, the book tells the story of how Jacobs was physically and sexually abused by her master and, in an attempt to escape the torture, hid for roughly seven years in a storeroom crawl space. Allyson returned home from school emotionally shaken by Jacobs's story. This was her first exposure to such a graphic slave narrative. Her response was outrage, anger, and sadness. She sympathized with the plight of Jacobs, but she was unable to empathize—to rid herself of what she perceived as the moral injustice done to this slave woman. She failed to fully understand the world of the nineteenth-century South in which Jacobs lived. My daughter developed an emotional connection with Jacobs, and I was glad that she did. She grew as a moral being through the reading of the narrative. But she was unable to understand Jacobs historically because sympathy kept getting in the way. This, of course, should be expected from a fourteen-year-old. Historical thinking of this nature, as I noted above, requires intellectual maturity.

The practice of empathy will inevitably lead to humility. It does so in one of three ways. First, an engagement with the past in all its breadth and fullness, the entry into such a "foreign country," should decenter us. It makes us realize our own smallness in the vast course of human history. The study of history is like being swallowed up in an immense ocean or field and losing oneself in its midst. It reminds me of the character of Jim Burden in Willa Cather's famous novel *My Antonia*. Upon arriving to the late nineteenth-century Nebraska frontier, Jim reflects on his own smallness in the vast fields of grass: "Between that earth and that sky I felt erased, blotted out." This is the essence of humility. Second, the practice of history cultivates humility because of the limited nature of the discipline. Since historians are often so far removed from the past they study, there is no way of ever knowing for sure that their interpretations are correct. Because of the "pastness of the past," the historian must come to grips with his or her own finiteness, realizing that he or she can never fully understand it in all its fullness and complexity. We have access to a record of the experience in the past but not the experience itself. Our attempt to feel the pain of the oppressed, the joy of the triumphant, or the love of country is limited by our distance from the events that we study.[25] Indeed, no one can be certain whether his or her explanations of the past are correct. Humility is ultimately an acknowledgment of one's limits and the realization that there are some things about the world that we cannot know fully. History, perhaps more than any other discipline, teaches this sense of limits. Third, history teaches humility in the sense that the past can sometimes shame us. In the process of seeing ourselves as part of a larger human story, we also see that the people who have gone before us were capable of tremendous atrocities. The story of human history is filled with accounts of slavery, violence, scientific backwardness, injustice, genocide, racism, and other dark episodes that might make us embarrassed to be part of the human race. If our fellow human beings can engage in such sad, wrong, or disgraceful acts, then what is stopping us from doing the same? History reminds us of the inherent weakness in the human condition and the very real possibility that our fellow human beings are capable of horrendous things. This should humble us, for "there but for the grace of God, go I."

A Case Study: An Encounter with Mormons

Brad Gregory is a historian at the University of Notre Dame. In a seminal article published in the journal *History and Theory*, Gregory tells the story of his undergraduate experience as a "Midwestern outsider" attending college in Utah and being exposed, for the first time in his life, to the teachings of Mormonism—the Church of Jesus Christ of Latter-day Saints (LDS). As a non-Mormon, Gregory quickly realized that he was an outsider at Utah State University, but he made every effort to understand the region's

25. Fulton, *From Judgment to Passion*, 424, 426.

dominant religion. Yet, as Gregory notes, "The more I comprehended LDS teachings—what the doctrines actually were and implied—the more *in*comprehensible did it seem that people actually believed them."[26] In his quest to figure out why Mormons believed what they did, Gregory came up with a few theories. Mormons were brainwashed. They were anti-intellectual. Perhaps they clung to their beliefs out of a fear of being ostracized from the Mormon community. Yet none of these theories seemed to help Gregory understand his new neighbors any better.

In the end, Gregory was forced to come to grips with the fact that Mormons were not like him. They were products of a different history, and thus, to this undergraduate, they were foreign. Gregory learned an important lesson in historical thinking through his encounter with members of the Church of Latter-day Saints. As he writes,

> I did not "get" Mormons, not despite but *because* of my explanations, since all of them implied that Mormonism is not what Mormons take it to be. It became apparent that if I wanted to "get" them, if I wanted to understand Mormons rather than to reduce their religion to something else—that is, if, as an outsider, I wanted to grasp as nearly as possible how they saw the world, why they did what they did, how their beliefs impinged on their social lives, political preferences, and cultural engagements—then there was no choice but to set aside what made sense to me and to endeavor to comprehend the relationship between their religious beliefs and their lives.[27]

Gregory concluded that Mormons did what they did because they believed that the LDS Church was the "one, true continuation and fulfillment of Christianity, revealed by God to his church through a series of latter-day prophets beginning with Joseph Smith in upstate New York in the early nineteenth century."[28]

When Gregory began to realize that Mormons behaved in the way they did—both in the past and the present—because they

---

26. Brad S. Gregory, "The Other Confessional History: On Secular Bias in the Study of Religion," *History and Theory* 45 (December 2006): 133.
27. Ibid.
28. Ibid.

believed the teachings of the LDS Church to be true, he began to think like a historian. He began to walk in the shoes of these people who were foreign to him and give agency to their voices. As far as I can tell, Gregory has never written any historical books or articles on the Church of Latter-day Saints, but if he did, what he learned from his college encounter with Mormons would be a very good start. In fact, empathy and humility are a very good start for any kind of venture in historical thinking, writing, and teaching.

Summing Up

We must always remember that the past is akin to a foreign country. Historians have the important task of visiting this world and explaining it to others through the books we write, the lectures we give, the lessons we plan, and the exhibits we curate. It is our responsibility to enter the past for the purpose of making sense of people, places, communities, and cultures that are different from our own. Historians are tour guides. It is important to always keep this in mind as you engage the past. Your success as a historian or a student of history will depend on how effectively you are able to use your research paper, essay, or presentation to bring lost worlds to life for your readers and hearers. But this will not be easy since our natural inclination—our "psychological condition at rest"—is to consume the past for our own purposes or try to remake the past in our own images. As an exercise in understanding, any serious study of the past requires us to attempt to humbly walk in the shoes of people who have inhabited this earth before us. This is why Wineburg has called the practice of historical thinking an "unnatural act."[29] As we will see in later chapters, it is this role of the historian—the role of a tour guide through foreign cultures—that has the best potential to transform our lives and the lives of those around us. It is our engagement with the otherness of these lost worlds that, ironically, prepares us well for life in the present.

29. Wineburg, *Historical Thinking and Other Unnatural Acts*.

4

Providence and History

IN THE EARLY 1650s, OLIVER CROMWELL, THE "LORD PRO-
tector" of England, believed that God wanted to use England to
usher in the end of the world as described in the New Testament
book of Revelation. As a Puritan, Cromwell thought that the will
of God would be accomplished if the English could remove the
Spanish from their various settlements in the Americas. To confirm
what he thought God was telling him, Cromwell consulted with
the well-respected New England Puritan clergyman John Cotton.
Cromwell specifically wanted to know if an English military attack
on the Spanish-controlled island of Hispaniola would conform
to God's will. Cotton not only affirmed that such an attack was
providentially ordained as a means of driving the Spanish Catholic
presence from America but also told Cromwell that it would serve
as a harbinger of the return of Jesus Christ. As historian Nicholas
Guyatt writes, "Cromwell believed fervently in the providential
significance of his Hispaniola invasion and this supernatural conviction blinded him to the military and political consequences of
failure." When Cromwell commenced his assault on the island
in the spring of 1655, his forces were badly defeated. Cromwell's

critics, using providential language of their own, claimed that the English defeat should be interpreted as a sign of God's punishment for the Lord Protector's tyrannical style of leadership.[1]

How does one interpret the will of God in such an incident? If no one in the seventeenth century could get it right, then why should we expect twenty-first-century historians to discern God's providence in such a matter? If God was using this invasion, as Cotton suggested, to usher in his kingdom, it certainly did not go the way God had planned it. Or perhaps God was using this event, as Cromwell's critics suggested, to humble him. Maybe God was using Cromwell's defeat to protect Catholicism in the New World against these Protestant invaders. The fact is, we just don't know. Those who lived in the early modern world often made bold statements about God's providence, but they could never be certain about what God was doing.

Let's look at a more contemporary story. Following college, Susan Fletcher pursued a master's degree in one of the best public history programs in the country. (Public historians preserve and communicate history to the public and work in such places as museums and archives.) She currently works as a public historian at the world headquarters of The Navigators, a Christian parachurch organization based in Colorado Springs. Susan's job is to manage the archives, present the history of The Navigators to interested parties, and interpret the history of Glen Eyrie, a beautiful conference ground of over 12,000 acres that was purchased by The Navigators' founder Dawson Trotman in 1953. (The Navigators moved their headquarters to this property at this time.) The centerpiece of Glen Eyrie is a twenty-two-room estate that was transformed into a castle by William Jackson Palmer, a nineteenth-century railroad magnate and founder of the city of Colorado Springs. When Susan first interviewed for her job at The Navigators, she was told that the organization was looking "for someone to document everything that God has been doing

1. Nicholas Guyatt, *Providence and the Invention of the United States, 1607–1876* (New York: Cambridge University Press, 2007), 40.

in the seventy-five-year history of the ministry." She cringed. She thought that if The Navigators wanted to attribute everything that happened in its history to divine providence, they would be better off hiring a theologian. "Real historians," even Christian historians, are not in the business of discerning God's actions in human history, she thought.

After four years on the job, Susan's ideas about providential history were seriously challenged. As she puts it, providence came "smashing into my own career as a public historian, shaking up my views on the legitimate types of public history." Susan was forced to revisit her thoughts on this subject following the Waldo Canyon wildfire that blazed through Colorado Springs in June 2012. The fire started less than a mile south of The Navigators' headquarters and Glen Eyrie. Both properties were evacuated. As Susan watched the spread of the fires on television, she heard "terrifying stories" of homes in close proximity to the Glen Eyrie Castle that were destroyed. She and the rest of The Navigators staff spent the evening in tears and prayer. It must have been a very long night. The following morning Susan learned that over three hundred homes surrounding Glen Eyrie had been destroyed by the fires, but Glen Eyrie had been untouched. As a good historian, Susan went right to work collecting stories related to the fire's impact (or lack of impact) on this beloved Colorado Springs landscape. Firefighters shared with her pictures, video, and oral testimonies relating to the wildfire's movement through the region. They told Susan that during the course of fighting the fire, they witnessed two-hundred-foot-high walls of flame heading straight for The Navigators' property only to make an immediate turn left away from the Christian retreat. As Susan looked at the thermal image maps from the fire, she said that "it looked like God had put his hands over our land and forbidden the fire from taking everything." Indeed The Navigators' property was surrounded on all sides by flames, and yet, with the exception of one cabin, it was left untouched.[2]

2. Susan Fletcher, "Providence and Public History," paper presented at the biennial meeting of the Conference on Faith and History, Wenham, MA, October 6, 2012. (Used with permission from the author.) Jack McQueeney, executive director

As a Christian, Susan could not help but believe that the Lord had answered her prayers and the prayers of the thousands of Navigators staff from around the world. It is hard not to agree with her. But should she interpret the Waldo Canyon wildfires differently when she was wearing her public historian's hat? She wondered whether these questions of God's providence would best be left to the theologians to interpret. Within her community of fellow Christians at The Navigators, it was easy to talk about God's providential sparing of Glen Eyrie, but how would she talk about this seemingly miraculous event to the nonbelieving public audiences that, as a public historian, she was charged to educate about this historic Colorado Springs property? Susan faced a conundrum that all Christian historians must face. How does one understand the relationship between providence and the study of history?[3]

The Doctrine of Providence

Like Oliver Cromwell, John Cotton, and Susan Fletcher, I believe in the doctrine of providence. God is the creator and the sustainer of the universe. As the Psalmist reminds us,

> The LORD builds up Jerusalem;
>   he gathers the exiles of Israel.
> He heals the brokenhearted
>   and binds up their wounds.
> He determines the number of the stars
>   and calls them each by name.
> Great is our Lord and mighty in power;
>   his understanding has no limit.
> The LORD sustains the humble
>   but casts the wicked to the ground.
> Sing to the LORD with grateful praise;

---

of Glen Eyrie, interviewed by a local television station said that firefighters described "unexplained fire behavior" that made "no earthly sense to us." See Bill Folsom, "Glen Eyrie Spared from Waldo Canyon Fire," KOAA.com News, July 12, 2012, www.koaa.com/news/glen-eyrie-spared-from-waldo-canyon-fire/#!prettyPhoto/0/.
    3. Ibid.

make music to our God on the harp.
He covers the sky with clouds;
   he supplies the earth with rain
   and makes the grass grow on the hills.
He provides food for the cattle
   and for the young ravens when they call.[4]

The Bible teaches us that all events fall under God's control. Indeed, as Psalm 103:19 affirms, "The LORD has established his throne in heaven, / and his kingdom rules over all." Whatever happens on this earth is providential. Everything happens because God wills it to happen. Providence is thus the doctrine of how God exercises his divine control over his creation. Or as historian Jon Boyd has put it, "Providence is the extension of the 'seven days' of creation all the way down through the reaches of history."[5]

When most Christians talk about divine providence, they do so in relation to their own lives or the lives of their loved ones. They want to know how their lives fit with the divine pattern for the universe.[6] This kind of providence, which historians and theologians describe as "special providence," differs from a more "general providence" in which one affirms that God is behind all events, ordering them and regulating them, without intruding into history in an identifiable pattern. When I refer to "providence," I am referring to the attempt by some students of the past not only to affirm a "special providence" but to interpret its manifestations in human history. Providence is a theological idea that is directly related to the character and behavior of God. History, however, is a discipline that seeks to explain the character and behavior of humans as they lived through time.[7] But the fact that providence is part of the theologian's toolbox, and not the historian's, has

---

4. Psalm 147:2–9.
5. Jonathan Tucker Boyd, "The Holy Hieroglyph: Providence and Historical Consciousness in George Bancroft's Historiography" (PhD dissertation, Johns Hopkins University, 1999), 11.
6. Paul Helm, *The Providence of God* (Downers Grove, IL: InterVarsity, 1993), 122–26.
7. Boyd, "Holy Hieroglyph," 35.

not stopped Christians from using it to enhance historical understanding. This chapter examines the relationship between God's providence and the historical task. It argues, from a Christian perspective, that providence is an unhelpful category in the interpretation of the past.

Providential History

Nearly every powerful empire or nation in history believed, in some sense, that its success was related to the guidance and intervention of a divine power. For centuries Christians have studied the past as a means of explaining the providence of God. Eusebius, the first true historian of the church, wrote his famous *Ecclesiastical History* in the fourth century as a vindication of Christianity. For Eusebius and many of his followers in the storied tradition of church history, the purpose of studying the past was to discern the will of God through the ages.[8] In this view, the exploration of the past becomes a subfield of theology. Its purpose is to communicate God's designs, not unlike how some of the historians of colonial New England wrote history for the purpose of glorifying God and revealing his handiwork. For example, early histories of America such as William Bradford's *Of Plymouth Plantation* (circa 1650) or Cotton Mather's *Magnalia Christi Americana* (1702) were written to explain God's providential ordering of the past. These works were designed to bring glory to the Creator for bestowing his special blessings on America and particularly New England. Bradford and Mather wrote with a sense of certainty about God's superintending hand. They believed it was possible to understand God's will and trace it over time.

Some of the leading advocates of historicism in nineteenth-century Germany, including Leopold von Ranke (referenced in the previous chapter), believed that God was at work in human

8. For a good discussion of providence and Christian scholarship, see Karl Giberson and Don Yerxa, "Providence and the Christian Scholar," *Journal of Interdisciplinary Studies* 11, no. 1/2 (1999): 123–40.

history and the historian had a responsibility to find the purposes of God in the past. This divine mission proved to be a significant motivating factor, even an inspiration, for doing historical work. In nineteenth-century America, especially before the American Civil War, several providential histories of the United States were written, none more magisterial than George Bancroft's ten-volume *History of the United States, from the Discovery of the American Continent* (1834–74). Bancroft was celebrated as a historian in the United States because he was trained in Germany, the center of professional historical scholarship in the West. His *History* was an attempt to write about the American past using footnotes and primary sources. It was also the first major effort at integrating theological convictions about God's sovereign rule of the universe with Ranke's German historicism. In good Rankean fashion, Bancroft sought to explain the American experience on its own terms. He wrote about causation and the interconnectedness of events, but he also claimed that all of these human movements were orchestrated by God. He suggested that the purpose of writing a multivolume history of the United States was "to follow the steps by which a favoring Providence, calling our institutions into being, has conducted the country to its present happiness and glory."[9]

With the establishment of the historical profession in the late nineteenth century, serious attempts at providential history began to fall out of favor. History became a science, and thus references to God's intrusion in human affairs were no longer considered a legitimate way of practicing the discipline. Today, few professional or academic historians would dare dabble in the kind of providential history that Bancroft did, but that has not stopped many Christians from trying. In fact, recent attempts at writing providential history are much more specific than Bancroft was about identifying God's actions in time.

For example, theologian Stephen Webb, writing in 2004, argued that Christians must believe in some form of specific providential

---

9. Cited in Boyd, "Holy Hieroglyph," ix. Boyd's dissertation is an attempt to show the compatibility between Bancroft's historicism and his providential commitments.

action because if they believed in only a general providence, "there would be no need to inquire into the specifics of a Christian reading of current events." He concludes, "While God's will is not revealed in rules that permit us to decode the hidden meaning of every historical event, God's will is given to us in a narrative that teaches us to read history according to a broad concrete plan." For Webb, the United States is at the center of that plan, and it is the Christian historian's task to search out God's "miraculous interventions" in the life of the nation.[10] Webb sounds a lot like a modern-day Mather or Bradford: God has a plan for America, we can know it, and we can thus interpret specific events with this knowledge in mind.

Steven Keillor, a creative historian who has made one of the best modern efforts at writing providential history, suggests that the doctrine of divine judgment is a useful way to understand the past. According to Keillor, many Christians have rushed to judgment about the meaning of historical events, but this does not mean that it is wrong to make an effort at discerning the will of God in the past. Through a close examination of pertinent passages in the Old and New Testaments, Keillor suggests that God has always judged nations for their sins and there is no reason to believe that he has stopped doing so today. Keillor takes a serious swipe at Christian historians in the academy for their failure to incorporate providence in their work. By neglecting to discuss the subject of God's judgment in human history, Keillor argues, Christian historians are neglecting a prominent theme in biblical theology. Keillor is more than willing to bring theological assertions about God's judgments into the practice of historical interpretation. For example, he argues that the War of 1812 was a judgment on the leadership (but not the people) of the United States for ungodly policies. The Civil War was a punishment on the United States for the institution of slavery. And the terrorist attacks on September 11, 2001, were a punishment on the United

10. Stephen H. Webb, *American Providence: A Nation with a Mission* (New York: Continuum, 2004), 4.

States for its greed and unbiblical use of military might during the Cold War. Such a quick summary of Keillor's argument does not do justice to his theological and historical reasoning; his work represents a serious effort to link the providence of God with the historical task.[11]

In 1994 the *Banner of Truth* magazine, a publication of the Calvinist publisher Banner of Truth Trust, criticized Yale University historian Harry Stout's biography of eighteenth-century revivalist George Whitefield, *The Divine Dramatist: George Whitefield and the Rise of Modern Evangelicalism*. Stout's biography was groundbreaking in its attempt to interpret Whitefield as a product of the eighteenth-century religious culture in which he lived and preached. Stout concluded that Whitefield's wild success as a revivalist could be explained by his effective use of print culture to disseminate his message and by his powerful and alluring speaking voice that was refined by his training in the theater. *Banner of Truth* writers harshly criticized Stout for not treating Whitefield's life through a providential lens. Iain Murray, the editorial director of the Banner of Truth Trust, wrote that Stout's portrayal of Whitefield was "hardly recognizable" because Stout did not acknowledge the role that God played in Whitefield's life. Murray accused Stout of writing history in such a way that "surrendered" to the "unregenerate" mind. Whitefield was successful, according to Murray, because the Holy Spirit guided his life and propelled his ministry. The Great Awakening did not happen because revivalists were effective at manipulating transatlantic developments in print and communication; it happened because God, in his sovereignty, decided to pour out his Holy Spirit on the people of the British Atlantic world. Murray and the folks at *Banner of Truth* wanted a providential history of Whitefield. Stout delivered a Whitefield couched "in the categories of social and cultural history rather than in the categories of theology and providence." Stout responded to the criticism by pointing to the limits of the historical enterprise. "Professional historians," he

11. Steven J. Keillor, *God's Judgments: Interpreting History and the Christian Faith* (Downers Grove, IL: InterVarsity, 2007).

wrote, "agree to settle for something less than ultimate explanations in the worlds that constitute our 'field.'" In other words, there are some metaphysical questions that go beyond the historian's vocation—even the Christian historian's vocation.[12]

The Light and the Glory

Providential history is alive and well in American evangelicalism. For most baby boomers, the name Peter Marshall triggers memories of the host of the 1970s game show *Hollywood Squares*, the straight man who kept Paul Lynde and Charlie Weaver in line. But a baby boomer raised in the evangelical subculture might recall Catherine Marshall's book *A Man Called Peter*, the biography of her husband, a Scottish-born Presbyterian minister who served two years as chaplain to the United States Senate before his death in 1949 at the age of forty-five. The story of Peter Marshall's journey from Ellis Island to Washington, and the faith that sustained him along the way, has inspired evangelical Christians for half a century. Catherine and Peter Marshall's son, also named Peter, is even more famous in the evangelical world than his father. With his friend David Manuel, he is the author of *The Light and the Glory*, one of the most widely read nonfiction Christian books of all time, with close to one million copies sold since it was first published by Fleming H. Revell in 1977. That *The Light and the Glory* is a book about early American history makes its sales even more impressive, but what makes the book worthy of reflection, more than thirty years after its publication, is its impact on hundreds of thousands of Christians, including students in homeschools and private Christian academies. Marshall and Manuel promote a "Christian view" of American history. *The Light and the Glory* was not the first (or the last) book to declare that the United States was founded as a "Christian nation," but it has certainly been the most influential.

12. The exchange of letters between Harry Stout and Iain Murray has been reprinted in "Evangelicals and the Writing of History," *Evangelical Studies Bulletin* 12, no. 1 (Spring 1995): 6–9.

It is easy to understand why *The Light and the Glory* has had such staying power in the evangelical world. While mainstream texts treat American history as if God did not exist, Marshall and Manuel offer a narrative of early American history focused on the sovereignty of God. The authors also tell their story in compelling prose. They occasionally inject their own voices into the narrative to explain how they crafted their argument through research and prayer.

The idea of a book about God's providential plan for the United States was conceived when Manuel, an editor at Doubleday Books, first heard Marshall speak on the topic at a Cape Cod church in the mid-1970s. Evangelicals were then beginning to awaken from a long political slumber. Jerry Falwell had formed the Moral Majority to "win the country back for God," and his army of pastors was preparing for a culture war. History would be one of the primary theaters in this war. As America celebrated its bicentennial, conservative Christians seized on the nation's newfound historical consciousness. The time had come for an alternative version of United States history, one that placed God at the center.

On this particular evening, Marshall was delivering an old-fashioned Puritan jeremiad. America had sinned. Abortion on demand, pornography, divorce, and unethical business practices offered indisputable evidence of moral decay. These social problems, he argued, were the inevitable product of a faulty view of America's historical identity. Citizens had failed to remember that the United States was one nation under God. If only Christians could recover God's special destiny for this country, America could be saved from divine punishment. The book that resulted from Marshall and Manuel's collaboration asserted that God deals with nations corporately in much the same way that he dealt with Old Testament Israel. The United States, from the time of its first settlement, was founded to show the rest of the world how to love God and neighbor. God had made a special covenant with this country, not unlike the covenant he made with the children of Jacob. Throughout its short history, America has occasionally lived up to this covenant, but at other times it has not. The study of the past presents a constant reminder of this unique and ongoing relationship between God and the United States and the role that all Americans, but especially Christians, play in making sure that divine favor rests on this land.

Marshall and Manuel begin with the story of Christopher Columbus, the "Christ bearer." Drawing from the spiritual musings recorded in Columbus's private writings, the authors conclude that Columbus was appointed by God to bring the gospel to the "heathen lands" of America. They begin with a question: "What if Columbus's discovery had not been accidental at all?" Indeed, what if he had "been called by God to found a Christian nation?"[13] Unfortunately, they say, Columbus's personal sins—greed and the lust for power and fame seem to be the most glaring—prevented him from carrying out this mission in the way that God had hoped he would. His quest for New World gold consumed him to the point that he turned a blind eye to his men's rape and murder of thousands of Native Americans.

Because of Columbus's numerous spiritual failures, Marshall and Manuel explain, God would have to look elsewhere for someone to prepare the way for his "New Promised Land." The real work of fulfilling the covenant was assigned to those whom God directed to the soil of New England. It was here that the Pilgrims of Plymouth and the Puritans of Massachusetts Bay developed a holy commonwealth, a "city on a hill," as Plymouth's Governor John Winthrop put it. The early Pilgrims were "locked in a life-or-death struggle with Satan himself. For this was the first time that the Light of Christ had landed in force on his continent, and if he did not throw them back into the sea at the beginning, there would be reinforcements."[14]

Marshall and Manuel describe how seventeenth-century New England Calvinists built communities with churches at their center. The communities celebrated family and were willing to sacrifice personal interest for the greater good. While it was necessary at

13. Peter Marshall and David Manuel, *The Light and the Glory* (Old Tappan, NJ: Fleming H. Revell, 1977), 18.
14. Ibid., 126.

times to remove divisive and arrogant members of their community, such as Roger Williams and Anne Hutchinson, such exclusion was needed to maintain spiritual purity. (Marshall and Manuel's chapter on Williams and Hutchinson is titled "The Pruning of the Lord's Vineyard.") The Pilgrims and Puritans were not perfect. Their cosmic engagement with the forces of evil often got the best of them. The City on a Hill faced a major crisis when second- and third-generation Puritans did not convert to Christ. Marshall and Manuel go on to say that Satan, at times, used witches to torment them and that God punished them for their sins with earthquakes and Indian wars. But God was always faithful even when the Puritans were not. In the end, despite the ever-present threat of evil and the much-to-be-expected consequences of human sin, God was carrying forth his plan, claim the authors. It was only a matter of time before Puritan New England became the United States of America. Because Marshall and Manuel sought facts from history that seemed to fit their thesis, their narrative is dominated by the story of early New England. Jamestown is covered and dismissed in one chapter, and other colonies (such as William Penn's experiment in Pennsylvania) and other religious movements (such as the Baptists and Anglicans) that shaped early American life are ignored.

The Light and the Glory argues that God was and is always on the side of freedom. The key Bible verse the authors use to support this view is Galatians 5:1: "For freedom Christ has set us free; stand firm therefore, and do not submit again to a yoke of slavery" (ESV). Such liberty, interpreted by the authors to mean freedom from political tyranny, is a God-given right that all humans must fight to preserve. The American Revolution was not only a just cause; it was the culmination of God's covenant relationship with America. The authors claim that Christian leaders, such as George Washington, became instruments to carry out God's will. The Declaration of Independence and the Constitution, documents based on Christian principles, were the means by which Americans reentered their covenant with God.

During the Revolutionary War, God intervened on numerous occasions to protect American forces from defeat and to preserve the Continental Army against what appeared to be insurmountable odds. For example, God saved the army from certain death during the "miracle" of the Valley Forge winter. For Marshall and Manuel, there is a direct connection between Washington's Christian faith and the survival of the troops at Valley Forge: "This, then, was the miracle at Valley Forge. That the men endured was indeed amazing to all who knew of their circumstances. But the reason they endured—the reason they believed in God's deliverance—was simple: they could believe, because their General *did* believe."[15]

Moreover, General Charles Lee's disagreement with Washington over how to attack the British Army was not merely a dispute over military strategy but an example of how Lee served the cause of Satan. "As long as Satan has men who have made total commitments to the magnification of their egos," the authors write, "he seldom has to intervene directly. Here, there was no need for satanic intervention at this crucial moment. . . . Charles Lee was doing just fine."[16]

Marshall and Manuel want us to see the hand of God at work in history. They seem to know when he is working and when he is not, based on what their sources—largely Puritans and Christian patriots—say. In this, they fail to exemplify the historian's necessary detachment from his or her subject. Just because historical actors believed something about the providential purposes behind the events they experienced does not mean they were correct in discerning the divine will. This would be the equivalent of future historians arguing that the events of September 11, 2001, were a punishment from God because their sources—certain prominent television preachers—said so.

Marshall and Manuel interpret the fog that rose in the East River on the morning of August 30, 1776, as God's direct intervention to aid Washington's midnight retreat from the British assault on the Continental Army's position on Brooklyn Heights. They describe the fog's rising as "the most amazing episode of divine intervention in the Revolutionary War."[17] They believe this because

15. Ibid., 322.
16. Ibid., 327.
17. Ibid., 313.

Washington, members of his staff, and many Continental soldiers described this event in terms of God's special protection of the army. Was God's providence evident in this event? American Christians certainly believed that it was, but I doubt whether an English Christian would have thought so. Who had the better insight into God's purposes? This is why it is so difficult to write providential history. An appeal to providence in a historical narrative like that of the East River fog of 1776 fails to help us better understand what happened on that day, and one of the historian's primary tasks is to aid our understanding of the past.

Can Christians claim to know God's purposes in history in the way that Marshall and Manuel suggest they can? I remain skeptical. As Jon Boyd has written, "If God's sovereignty extends over all and his providence comprises all events, what good does it do to denominate some events as more providential than others?"[18] For example, many eighteenth-century Protestants (as well as many contemporary Protestants) believed that God intervened in human history on the side of Martin Luther and his fellow Reformers. Is this true? Perhaps. But to suggest that the Reformation was an example of God's providential intervention in the affairs of humankind is also to suggest that God was not overseeing human history before he had to "intervene" at Wittenberg in October 1517. Similarly, does it really help our understanding of the Revolutionary War to claim, as Marshall and Manuel do, that during the American invasion of Canada, "Divine Providence, it seemed, was dispensed—or withheld—in direct relationship to how close an individual or body of men was to the center of God's perfect will"?[19] Can God's providence be "withheld"? What *is* God's "perfect will" in matters such as this?

The Mystery of God and the Historian's Vocation

For Christians who believe in divine providence, the study of history certainly presents a conundrum. As believers, we want to know

18. Boyd, "Holy Hieroglyph," 245.
19. Marshall and Manuel, *Light and the Glory*, 295.

God's will for our lives. We spend time in prayer and meditation trying to discern what he is calling us to do in the circumstances of our lives. We often look back on our lives and reflect on the way the Lord has led us. So if we try to discern providence in our own spiritual lives, what is wrong with trying to do the same thing with the most important events of the past? Should our historical methods, to quote Christian scholars Karl Giberson and Donald Yerxa, "ignore God"? Where is God in history? These are tough questions indeed.[20]

Providential historians must be willing to reconcile their certainty about God's plan for America with St. Paul's words in 1 Corinthians 13:12: "For now we see in a mirror dimly, but then face to face. Now I know in part; then I shall know fully, even as I have been fully known" (ESV). Books like *The Light and the Glory* often offer a simple and direct providential reading of American history that assumes an understanding of the secret things of God, things that sinful people cannot fathom outside of the Scriptures. God is indeed the "blessed and only Ruler, the King of kings and Lord of lords," but he also "lives in unapproachable light, whom no one has seen or can see" (1 Tim. 6:15–16). And let's not forget Isaiah 55:8–9: "'For my thoughts are not your thoughts, / neither are your ways my ways,' / declares the LORD. / 'As the heavens are higher than the earth, / so are my ways higher than your ways / and my thoughts than your thoughts.'"[21]

Granted, if I were to get up from my word processor, cross the street to my neighbor's house, and steal his big screen television, I would have a pretty good sense, based on the teachings of the Bible, that God would be displeased with my behavior. But what if as I was walking to my neighbor's house to rob him, I tripped, fell down, and broke my ankle. Did God allow me to trip in order

20. Giberson and Yerxa, "Providence and the Christian Scholar"; Tim Stafford, "Whatever Happened to Christian History?," *Christianity Today*, April 2, 2001, www.christianitytoday.com/ct/2001/april2/1.42.html?start=9.
21. Mark Noll, "Traditional Christianity and the Possibility of Historical Knowledge," in *Religious Advocacy and American History*, ed. Bruce Kuklick and D. G. Hart (Grand Rapids: Eerdmans, 1997), 50; Arthur S. Link, "The Historian's Vocation," *Theology Today* 19 (April 1962): 88.

to stop me from breaking into my neighbor's house? For many Christians, the answer would be an unqualified yes. But what if God had some other plan, or multiple plans, for my clumsiness? Again, we just don't know. Augustine is helpful here. In book 20 of *The City of God against the Pagans*, he reminds us what Christians can and cannot know about God's work in the world. We can be confident, from what the Scriptures teach us, in the hope of Christ's return and final judgment. History will end with the glorious triumph of the Son of God. But as we live with this hope, we must be cautious about trying to pinpoint the specific plan of God in history. We must avoid trying to interpret what is hidden from us or what is incomprehensible, because our understanding is so limited. As Augustine writes,

> There are good men who suffer evils and evil men who enjoy good things, which seems unjust, and there are bad men who come to a bad end, and good men who arrive at a good one. Thus, the judgments of God are all the more inscrutable, and His ways past finding out. We do not know, therefore, by what judgment God causes or allows these things to pass.[22]

The Swiss theologian Karl Barth, who had a strong view of God's providential ordering of the world, warned us about trying to get too specific in explaining the ways in which God's work manifests itself in the world. As Webb notes, Barth went so far in "advising restraint, modesty, and caution in the use of this doctrine that he nearly undermines his own insistence on its importance."[23] The great Protestant Reformer Martin Luther was also clear about what Christians can and cannot know about the will of God in human history. Luther always erred on the side of mystery: God is transcendent and sovereign; humans are sinful and finite. During the Heidelberg Disputation, Luther was quite candid about the human quest to understand God's purposes in the world. "That person," Luther wrote, "does not deserve to be called a theologian

22. Augustine, *The City of God against the Pagans*, ed. R. W. Dyson (Cambridge: Cambridge University Press, 1998), book 20, chap. 2, 968.
23. Webb, *American Providence*, 97–98.

who looks upon the invisible things of God as though they were clearly perceptible in those things which have actually happened."[24]

Invoking providence must always be done with caution, especially for the historian, who is commissioned with the job of telling the story of the past accurately. We need to avoid what Ambrose Bierce, in his *Devil's Dictionary*, gave as the definition of "providence": an idea that is "unexpectedly and consciously beneficial to the person so describing it."[25] If our attempts at trying to understand what God is doing in our own individual lives are at best provisional, it must be exponentially more difficult to know what God was doing on a more macro or universal level in human history (apart from fulfilling the promise of his Word). As Paul Helm argues, "The Bible stresses that none of us knows what a day may bring forth, and that our lives cannot be planned definitively but are subject to the will of God. Any other attitude is unwarranted, and verges on the blasphemous, for by it we presume to take into our own hands matters which God keeps in his."[26]

Christian historians would do better to approach their task with a sense of God's transcendent mystery, a healthy dose of humility, and a hope that one day soon, but not now, we will all understand the Almighty's plans for the nations. We should again take comfort in the words of Augustine: "When we arrive at that judgment of God, the time of which in a special sense is called the Day of Judgment, . . . it will become apparent that God's judgments are entirely just."[27] The will of God in matters such as these often remains a mystery. As theologian Charles Mathewes notes, "The lesson of providence is not that history can be finally solved, like a cryptogram, but that it must be endured, inhabited as a mystery which we cannot fully understand from the inside, but which we cannot

24. Cited in Douglas A. Sweeney, "Taking a Shot at Redemption," *Books and Culture: A Christian Review*, May 1, 1999, 6.

25. *The Collected Works of Ambrose Bierce*, 12 vols. (New York: Neale, 1909–12), 7:269–70.

26. Helm, *Providence of God*, 129.

27. Augustine, *City of God*, book 20, chap. 2, 968.

escape of our own powers."[28] The primary task of the historian is to describe the way that humans—created by God in his image—have "endured" and "inhabited" the mysteries of life. History is more about the study of humans than it is about the study of God. As the noted historiographer R. G. Collingwood put it,

> The work of providence in history is recognized . . . but recognized in such a way which leaves nothing for man to do. One result of this is that historians . . . fell into the error of thinking that they could forecast the future. Another result is that in their anxiety to detect the general plan of history, and their belief that this plan was God's and not man's, they tended to look for the essence of history outside of history itself, by looking away from man's actions in order to detect the plan of God; and consequently the actual detail of human actions became for them relatively unimportant, and they neglected that prime duty of the historian, a willingness to bestow infinite pains on discovering what actually happened.[29]

Summing Up

Is providential history possible? I am often asked this question by my students and others whom I encounter in church or speaking engagements. The distinguished evangelical historian Mark Noll once told *Christianity Today* that while he believed "good providential history could be done," he had yet to "see good examples of it." He added that providential history only made sense to "people who already shared your specific religious position. If someone said the Reformation was God's way of bringing about a reform in the church, I knew that person wasn't a Catholic."[30] I can imagine that a form of providential history might be useful in helping a

28. Charles Mathewes, *A Theology of Public Life* (New York: Cambridge University Press, 2007), 40–41.
29. R. G. Collingwood, *The Idea of History* (Oxford: Oxford University Press, 1946), 50–51.
30. Stafford, "Whatever Happened to Christian History?" Noll elaborates on providential history further in his *Jesus Christ and the Life of the Mind* (Grand Rapids: Eerdmans, 2011), 85–98.

religious congregation or some other community of Christians make sense of the way that God has led them through the days, months, and years. Such a providential history would obviously be celebratory in nature and be written to encourage the faithful with the things that God has done. But such providential history must always be written with a sense of humility and a commitment to the mystery of God. It must be seasoned with words like "perhaps" or "maybe" or "might." Or as theologian N. T. Wright has argued, "When Christians try to read off what God is doing even in their own situations, such claims always have to carry the word *perhaps* about with them as a mark of humility and of the necessary reticence of faith. That doesn't mean that such claims can't be made, but that they need to be made with a 'perhaps' which is always inviting God to come in and say, 'Well, actually, no.'"[31]

In the end, the writer of providential history must resist the temptation to bow to the gods of modernity—gods who want to scientifically decipher the workings of the divine and claim to know, with a degree of Enlightenment certainty, the will of a sovereign God who created the modern world and will end it when he sees fit. Until then, we see through a glass darkly.

31. Wright quoted in Stafford, "Whatever Happened to Christian History?"

5

Christian Resources
for the Study of the Past

THOUGH I AM SKEPTICAL ABOUT THE USE OF PROVIDENCE
as a tool of historical investigation, there are still plenty of
resources in the Christian tradition that historians might
find useful in doing their work. If you are a Christian, you may
have already begun to think about how your faith intersects with
the study of the past. I hope that this chapter will aid you in the
process. What follows is not meant to engage the ongoing debate
over whether or not there is a distinctly "Christian" view of history. I will leave that to my friends who represent the Reformed
tradition.[1] As I have argued elsewhere, I prefer to understand the
relationship between faith and historical scholarship in terms of
a theology of work. The historian's calling is driven more by the
ways in which he or she strives to practice his or her craft in a
Christian manner than it is by the production of a particularly

---

1. For the so-called Calvin School of historiography, see Douglas Sweeney,
"Taking a Shot at Redemption," *Books and Culture*, May/June 1999, www.books
andculture.com/articles/1999/mayjun/9b3043.html.

"Christian" piece of scholarship.[2] Yet there are certain beliefs and practices—the *imago Dei*, the reality of sin, the incarnation, and, to a lesser extent, Christian moral reflection—that help historians to make sense of the human condition.

The *Imago Dei*

As we saw in the last chapter, historians are not in the business of studying God; they are in the business of studying humans. But those committed to the Judeo-Christian tradition believe that God has created humans. In the opening chapters of the Old Testament book of Genesis, we learn more about what that means. One central theme in the Genesis creation story is the affirmation that humans are created in the image of God (*imago Dei* in Latin). Consider Genesis 1:26–27:

> Then God said, "Let us make mankind in our image, in our like- ness, so that they may rule over the fish in the sea and the birds in the sky, over the livestock and all the wild animals, and over all the creatures that move along the ground." So God created mankind in his own image, in the image of God he created them; male and female he created them.

That God created us in his image, that we are the highest form of his creation, implies that all human beings have inherent dignity and worth independent of their actions and behavior. Because we are made in the likeness of our creator and thus share, in some fashion, the divine image, human life is precious and sacred. There are no villains in history. While people have been created with freedom, and are thus capable of performing villainous or sinful acts, even the most despicable human subject bears the image of God and thus has inherent value in God's eyes.

If life is indeed sacred and valuable, then Christians have a respon- sibility to celebrate and protect it. Scholars debate the particular

2. John Fea, "Confessions of a 'Pile-man': Work and the Scholarly Task of the Christian Historian," *Network Communique: The Newsletter of the Lilly Fellows Program in Humanities and the Arts* 14 (Spring 2001): 5–7.

meaning of the *imago Dei* for our lives, but most would agree that it provides a foundation for Christian social teaching. The belief that we are created in the image of God should translate into our convictions about war, abortion, capital punishment, and the care of the poor. It also informs the Christian's understanding of human equality. If we are all created in God's image, then discrimination based on race, color, social condition, language, or religion violates God's design for humans. And the *imago Dei* should also inform the way a Christian does history. This doctrine should guide us in the kinds of stories we tell about the people whom we come across when visiting the "foreign country" that is the past. It should shape the way we teach the past, write about the past, and interpret the past.

An approach to the past informed by an affirmation of the *imago Dei* can make the Christian historian's work compatible with some of the best scholarship that the historical profession has to offer. Let me illustrate this from my own subdiscipline, the study of colonial American history. Lately, historians have been complicating the very definition of what we have traditionally called "colonial America." Recent scholarship on the history of the North American continent between 1500 and 1800 has suggested that "colonial America" is a loaded phrase. For most of my students, "colonial America" is equivalent to the "thirteen colonies"—those individual settlements that came together in 1776 to rebel against England and form the United States of America. When I ask them why we should study the colonies, they inevitably answer by saying something about the importance of understanding the reasons for the American Revolution and the founding of the United States. For most of them, the purpose of studying the colonial period is to locate the seeds of their nation—as if these seeds were somehow planted in the soil of Jamestown and Plymouth, were watered through a host of seventeenth- and eighteenth-century events, and finally blossomed in the years between the resistance to the Stamp Act (1765) and the writing of the Declaration of Independence (1776). The colonial period thus becomes part of the grand civics lesson that is the American history survey course.

This approach to teaching history has demographic implications. Who are the most important actors in the stories we tell about the

American colonies? Since the United States survey course has always been taught as a way of producing good American citizens, the most important people and events will be those who contributed to the forging of a new nation. In this view, the worth of particular humans living during this period, or the degree of prominence that these humans will have in the stories we tell about the period, is based on the degree to which they contributed to the creation of the United States rather than their dignity as human beings created in God's image. For example, we might give short shrift to humans living in North America who did not contribute in obvious ways to the founding of the American republic. We all know the usual suspects: Native Americans, women, slaves, and anyone not living in the British colonies. But if the colonial period is understood less as a prelude to the American Revolution and more as a vital and fascinating period worthy of study on its own, then these marginalized historical actors become more important and our teaching becomes more comprehensive, inclusive, and, according to recent scholarship, historically accurate.

Consider Alan Taylor's *American Colonies*, a history of colonial America published in 2002. For Taylor, a Pulitzer Prize–winning historian, the colonies should not be studied solely for how they served as the necessary forerunner to the events of the American Revolution. Rather, they should be studied for the story of European imperial expansion in North America and for the impact that such expansion had on whites, natives, and slaves. The changes that this expansion brought to the lives of ordinary people, Taylor argues, were the real "revolution" that took place on the continent between 1500 and the turn of the nineteenth century. For Taylor, European expansion did more to change the lives of the inhabitants of North America than did the hostilities between the British colonies and the mother country in the years leading up to 1776. This was a social revolution, not a political one.[3]

Taylor turns the concept of the "New World" on its head, suggesting that the colonial expansion of Europe throughout the

3. Alan Taylor, *American Colonies: The Settling of North America* (New York: Penguin, 2002), x–xii.

Atlantic (and Pacific) basin brought profound changes to the Indian populations who were already there, the Africans who would arrive as slaves, and even the Europeans themselves. The American colonies were diverse and "multicultural" places. Africans, Indians, the French, the English, the Spanish, the Dutch, and even the Russians in the Pacific Northwest encountered one another in this new world. And everyone involved in this encounter was forced to adjust and adapt. All of these groups helped to create a truly global economy and, conversely, were profoundly influenced by global economic trends. Slaves were shipped as commodities to the Americas. Indians and their wars had an effect on European markets for skins and furs, even as Indian culture itself was changed by access, if not addiction, to British, French, and Spanish consumer commodities. Such engagement also had environmental consequences as both Europeans *and Indians* overworked the land. European disease changed the indigenous populations of North America forever. As for the United States, the colonial period was important for the way all of these "colonies," with their very diverse backgrounds and cultures, assimilated over time into one national story. The British colonists and their gripes with Parliament and the king were only one part, albeit a very important part, of this larger narrative.[4]

Some might argue that Taylor's analysis of the colonial period is driven more by politics than by good historical practice. By including the stories of Native Americans and slaves in his narrative, Taylor is engaging in political correctness. He is giving short shrift to the white Europeans who planted the American colonies. According to such a critique, *American Colonies* is just another example of the left-wing historical takeover of American history. Its interpretation is akin to the way liberal historians tried to rewrite our nation's past in the 1990s during the controversy over the National History Standards that we discussed in chapter 2. But what if we looked at the changes in the field of colonial American history, as portrayed most forcefully in Taylor's *American Colonies*, from a theological perspective rooted in the belief that we are all created in the image of

4. Ibid.

God and thus have inherent dignity and worth? If we view colonial America, or any period in American history for that matter, from God's eyes, then we get a very different sense of whose voices should count in the stories we tell. To put this differently, *everyone's* voice counts, regardless of whether that person or group contributed to the eventual formation of the United States. Now, of course, certain white Europeans—such as the founding fathers—will appear prominently in our accounts of the American Revolution and its coming, but Whig history too often only celebrates the winners, the beneficiaries of liberty and progress, or the most privileged figures in the history of Western civilization. Whig history neglects anyone who does not fit this mold, and it fails to consider the *imago Dei* as a legitimate category of historical interpretation.

Theologian Miroslav Volf reminds us that "God sees each human being concretely, the powerful no less than the powerless. God notes not only their common humanity, but also their *specific histories*, their particular psychological, social, and embodied selves with their specific needs."[5] What might this reality look like in our historical writing and thinking about the past? On closer examination, much of this new scholarship in colonial American history seems to be more compatible with Christian teaching about human dignity than the nationalistic narratives that have dominated much of the nineteenth and early part of the twentieth century and which still have influence today. A history grounded in a belief in the *imago Dei* will not neglect the elite and privileged members of society, but it will also demand a fundamental reordering of the stories we tell about the human actors we meet in the past.

The Reality of Human Sin

In addition to having dignity and worth, we were created by God with freedom. Every human person, created in the image of God, has the natural right to be recognized as a responsible and free

5. Miroslav Volf, *Exclusion and Embrace: A Theological Exploration of Identity, Otherness, and Reconciliation* (Nashville: Abingdon, 1996), 222, emphasis added.

being. This is an important part of God's image within us. The freedom to make choices with our lives can lead us toward a life of communion with God, but it can also lead us into sin. Humans all through history have made the choice to prefer themselves over God. Christians believe that because of the fall, the image of God in all of us has been tarnished by sin. Our natural inclination is toward selfishness and the pursuit of our wants and desires rather than the pursuit of God or love of neighbor. Creation, the world in which we live, is broken. Theologian Scot McKnight reminds us that the Greek word for "image" (as in the "image of God") is *eikōn*. We all share God's *eikōn*, but after the fall we have become cracked *eikōns* in need of the redemption that Jesus Christ offers.[6] All humans are implicated in the sin of Adam. Saint Paul put it best in Romans 5: "Through the disobedience of the one man the many were made sinners" and "sin entered the world through one man, and death through sin, and in this way death came to all people, because all sinned" (vv. 19, 12). Jesus Christ's sacrificial death and resurrection on our behalf has provided a way to restore our true image, but sin still rears its ugly head in our lives and in the lives of those around us. The sinfulness of humans means that we live in a world filled with brokenness, injustice, and violence.

How might the reality of human sin influence our work as historians? Herbert Butterfield, a twentieth-century philosopher of history, informed us that "if there is any region in which the bright empire of the theologians and the more murky territory of the historians happen to meet and overlap, we shall be likely to find it at those places where both types of thinkers have to deal with human nature."[7] Historian George Marsden adds, "Of all traditional Christian teachings the doctrine of original sin or of pervasive human depravity has the most empirical verification. The modern world, rather than undercutting this doctrine, seems increasingly

6. Scot McKnight, *40 Days Living the Jesus Creed* (Brewster, MA: Paraclete Press, 2008), 31.
7. Herbert Butterfield, *Christianity and History* (London: Fontana Books, 1957), 40.

to confirm it."[8] Indeed, anyone who studies the past realizes that there are no heroes in history. While people may perform heroic acts, all humans are tainted by sin and are susceptible to acting in ways that preference themselves over others and God. Historians understand, perhaps better than most, the reality of the pain, suffering, injustice, anger, and vice brought on by sin. In other words, they understand the tragic dimensions of life.

I often tell my Christian students that it is very difficult to understand historical figures like Nero, Caligula, Adolf Hitler, Joseph Stalin, and Pol Pot without a robust understanding of sin. But a belief in human depravity and the sinfulness of this world can have a much deeper effect on the way we approach the past that goes beyond its mere use as a tool for pointing out the source of injustice and oppression. A belief in the reality of sin should provide us with a healthy skepticism about movements in the past committed to utopian ends, unlimited progress, or idealistic solutions to the problems of this world. This, of course, does not mean that we should stop working toward these ends, but history certainly teaches us that we live in a broken world that will not be completely fixed on this side of eternity. Similarly, a belief in depravity helps us to better explain the human condition—the restlessness, the search for meaning, and the prideful ambition that has defined much of the past, especially in the modern era. Augustine was quite correct when he opened his *Confessions* with the famous words, "Our hearts are restless until they rest in you."

In the same way that a belief in the *imago Dei* should shape the stories that we tell about the past, a belief in sin should influence the process by which we craft our narratives of the human experience. Let me again draw on my own expertise as an American historian to illustrate this point. As we have already seen, the study of American history has always served a civic function in the United States. Schoolchildren learn American history for the purpose of becoming informed and patriotic citizens. What has

8. George M. Marsden, "Human Depravity: A Neglected Explanatory Category," in *Figures in the Carpet: Finding the Human Person in the American Past*, ed. Wilfred M. McClay (Grand Rapids: Eerdmans, 2007), 16.

resulted from this approach to teaching history is a skewed view of the American experience that celebrates certain heroic figures to the neglect of others. Such an approach also focuses on American greatness as defined by the patriotic designers of school textbooks. In such a curriculum, American nationalism triumphs over the stories chronicling those moments when the United States failed or when it acted in ways that might be considered unjust. Such an approach to American history is not only one-sided; it also fails to recognize the theological truth that all earthly kingdoms and nations are flawed when compared to the kingdom of God. While the stories we tell about the United States should certainly not neglect the moments that make us feel good about our country, we should also not be surprised when we encounter stories that may lead us to hang our heads in collective shame. While such a whitewashing of American history is quite popular these days among those on the political or cultural Right, those who occupy a place on the political or cultural Left can also ignore the realities of human sin on the subjects or individuals that they find to be inspirational. Yet, as Marsden reminds us, it is "a sign of maturity" when "representatives of a group can write history that takes into account that members of that group are flawed humans like everyone else. In the long run the most convincing histories will be those that portray their protagonists with faults as well as virtues."[9]

The reality of sin in this world also affects what we can know about the past. As Mark Noll argues, "The doctrine of the Fall and the resultant depravity of human nature suggest that the human moral condition obscures vision, presumably for historical as well as moral reasoning." Ephesians 4:18 teaches us that sin darkens the understanding. Indeed, as we learned in the previous chapter on God's providence, we "see through a glass dimly."[10] These limitations on human knowledge should humble historians and serve as a caution against the temptation to claim, particularly in the

9. Marsden, "Human Depravity," 31.
10. Mark Noll, "Traditional Christianity and the Possibility of Historical Knowledge," in *Religious Advocacy and American History*, ed. Bruce Kuklick and D. G. Hart (Grand Rapids: Eerdmans, 1997), 45–46.

public sphere, that we speak with an authoritative cer
what happened in the past.

An Incarnational Approach to the Past

Some of the most interesting work on the relationship between
truth and the possibility of historical knowledge has been written
by Christian historians. Noll of the University of Notre Dame has
approached the study of the past through the doctrines of creation
and the incarnation of Jesus Christ.[11] A belief in a creator God,
as set forth in historical statements of orthodox Christian belief,
such as the Apostles' Creed, the Nicene Creed, and the Chalce-
donian Creed, implies that there is inherent value in studying the
works of his creation, including the history of interactions among
humans who have inhabited the created world through time. An
incarnational approach to history affirms that God revealed himself
most completely in the material world (John 1). It suggests that
the material world is important because it is the locus in which the
Word became flesh. The stuff of earth thus merits scholarly and
intellectual consideration in all its realms. Belief in Christ and his
redemptive work on our behalf requires obedience and submission
to God's commands in every aspect of our lives. To confess the
gospel naturally results in the acknowledgment of God's sovereignty
over all of creation and all fields of inquiry. As Noll writes,

> Since the reality of Jesus Christ sustains the world and all that
> is in it, so too should the reality of Jesus Christ sustain the most
> wholehearted, unabashed, and unembarrassed efforts to understand
> the world and all that is in it. . . . Whatever is true of the world in
> general must also be true for those parts of the world that empha-
> size intellectual life. The light of Christ illuminates the laboratory,
> his speech is the fount of communication, he makes possible the
> study of humans in all their interactions, he is the source of all
> life, he provides the wherewithal for every achievement of human

11. This section relies heavily on Mark A. Noll, *Jesus Christ and the Life of
the Mind* (Grand Rapids: Eerdmans, 2011).

f all that is beautiful. He is, among his
t of the Academic Road.[12]

ɪ, we can have confidence in our ability
ike Peter Hoffer (referenced in chap. 1
ɪe historian's paradox"), Noll affirms
ippened out there long ago" and that
lity to find out what it was. But unlike
·om an overtly Christian perspective,
ɪ·υɪɪ unuerstanas the possibility of historical knowledge through the
teachings of the historical Christian creeds. Creation and the incarnation offer a reason for paying attention to all of the past, whether
it is relevant or not. Writing in the context of the postmodernist
challenge to historical truth, Noll concludes that "believers worried
about the fragility of historical knowledge can take heart from the
assurance that the wherewithal for human cultural activity . . . was
created by God. . . . If the Bible affirms that the creation is good, it
is reasonable to assume that we may know that it is good, and, even
more basically, that we may know it."[13] In other words, our work as
historians need not be fruitless. Indeed, the study of the past in all
its fullness becomes an act of pursuing the experiences of humans—
God's highest order of creation. And when we look deeply into the
human experience, we are brought face-to-face with the *imago Dei*,
the brokenness of creation, and the world in which God chose to
manifest himself most fully in the person of Jesus Christ. History
thus becomes an act of worship. It should cause us to praise God
for the goodness of creation and bow in humility over the failure of
humans to live up to his highest demands on our lives.

The Role of Moral Reflection in Historical Work

Should historians cast judgment on the past? Is this part of their
vocation? Some believe that the past must be critiqued from the

12. Noll, *Jesus Christ*, 22.
13. Ibid., 80–81.

perspective of Christian orthodoxy—a body of biblical teaching and church tradition that has guided Christians in judging right from wrong since the beginning of the church. This approach to history allows us to offer ethical judgments on characters from the past, the ideas they defended, and the movements they were involved with. Indeed, the past provides us with moral lessons, making the historian—sometimes overtly, but most times subtly (but no less powerfully)—a critic by nature. Historian Philip Gleason has argued that historians have a threefold task: to explain what happened, to ask why it happened, and to ask if what happened was "good." Those who embrace this vision of history find it imperative to add this moral dimension to their study of the past, one that is informed by their Christian convictions.[14]

Let's examine Gleason's approach to history from the perspective of the American Revolution. We have plenty of evidence from the eighteenth century to conclude that the American Revolution happened. Over the course of about a decade (roughly between 1765 and 1776), the British-American colonies grew increasingly dissatisfied in their relationship with England, eventually leading to a colonial rebellion, a declaration of independence, and a war. When it was all over, the United States of America, a nation that existed independent of England, had been born. This information would fall comfortably under Gleason's first point, namely, that the historian is responsible for explaining what happened.

But it is nearly impossible for a historian to provide an explanation of what happened without dabbling in some degree of interpretation. The very arrangement of the so-called facts into a compelling story is itself an act of interpretation. Historians of the American Revolution will decide which facts to include in their narrative or how much emphasis should be placed on, for

14. Philip Gleason, *Keeping the Faith: American Catholicism Past and Present* (Notre Dame, IN: Notre Dame University Press, 1987), 216–20. For a further discussion of these issues, see Grant Wacker, "Understanding the Past, Using the Past: Reflections on Two Approaches to History," in Kuklick and Hart, *Religious Advocacy*, 160–66.

example, the resistance to the Stamp Act versus the resistance to the Townshend duties. In the process, these historians are making a case for *why* the American Revolution happened when it did. They are beginning to apply the Five C's of historical thinking to their work. Questions will arise. Was the American Revolution the product of economic resistance to British taxation by ordinary people in major port cities like Boston, New York, Philadelphia, and Charleston? Or did the American Revolution happen because educated men—the so-called founding fathers—offered radical political solutions to what they believed to be British tyranny? Or was it both?

The recitation of facts and the interpretation of those facts fall squarely within the realm of the historian's work. But Gleason wants to push the vocation of the historian even further. He wants us to ask whether or not the American Revolution was "good." One way of getting at this question is to ask whether the colonial rebellion that formed the United States of America was justified. At this point, historians move from being chroniclers or interpreters of past events to moral arbiters. The questions that they ask can no longer be answered through archival research or the close examination of primary sources. Such questions can only be answered by an appeal to some kind of moral system.[15] Is it ever right to rebel against government authority? Is war ever justified? And if so, how should we evaluate a war waged over high taxes or lack of political representation?

Historians have long been divided over these kinds of moral questions. It is important to remember that until the professionalization of the study of history in the late nineteenth century, historians had no qualms about imposing moral judgments on the past. History was written to tell the story of winners and losers in an epic struggle for power, to critique or praise the nation, or to reveal the hand of God at work in the world. For example,

15. Historian David Hackett Fischer uses the phrase "the fallacy of metaphysical questions" to describe an "attempt to resolve a nonempirical problem by empirical means." Fischer, *Historians' Fallacies: Toward a Logic of Historical Thought* (New York: Harper & Row, 1970), 12.

the Roman historian Tacitus claimed that the "highest function" of studying the past was to "let no worthy action be uncommemorated, and to hold out the reprobation of posterity as a terror to evil words and deeds."[16] His goal was not merely to chronicle what happened in the past but to glorify the "worthy" and condemn those who were "evil." The professionalization of history in the late nineteenth century made history into a science. Historians were now required to be detached observers, chroniclers, and interpreters of the past. With the rise of the research university and the creation of academic disciplines, historians resisted the temptation to moralize about the events and people of the past. Based on a new division of scholarly labors, historians argued that it was their responsibility simply to tell and explain "what happened." They would leave the moral pontificating to their colleagues in religion, theology, and ethics.[17] Or as historian David Hackett Fischer argues, the exercising of moral opinions in historical writing is "inconsistent with a serious and disciplined empirical inquiry into what actually happened. It would make history a hand-maiden of moral philosophy."[18]

As the twentieth century progressed, some of the world's most prominent historians came out strongly in opposition to the idea that historians should make moral judgments. In 1954 Marc Bloch (1886–1944), the esteemed founder of the Annales School, referred to "that . . . satanic enemy of true history: the mania for making judgments." E. H. Carr (1892–1982), the noted historian of the Russian Revolution and the Soviet Union, proclaimed that historians who dabble in the "unhistorical" practice of making judgments "renounce" their vocation.[19] Herbert Butterfield, the Christian historiographer, believed that to make moral judgments in history is to engage in "the most useless and unproductive of all forms of

16. Cited in ibid., 80.
17. Richard T. Vann, "Historians and Moral Evaluations," *History and Theory* 43 (December 2004): 6.
18. Fischer, *Historians' Fallacies*, 78.
19. Beverly Southgate, "'A Pair of White Gloves': Historians and Ethics," *Rethinking History* 10 (March 2006): 52; Henry Steele Commager, "Should the Historian Make Moral Judgments?," *American Heritage* 17 (February 1996): 92.

reflection."[20] Henry Steele Commager (1902–98), one of the greatest American historians of the twentieth century, described moral judgment in history as a "futile" exercise. He argued that the practice of praising America's commitment to freedom or castigating its toleration of slavery ultimately offended his readers:

> The assumption behind this expectation is that the reader has no mind of his own, no moral standards, no capacity to exercise judgment; . . . he depends upon the historian to do this for him. Are those mature enough to read serious histories really so obtuse that they cannot draw conclusions from facts that are submitted to them? Is there really a danger that students will yearn for slavery or rejoice in the inquisition or admire Philip II or Adolf Hitler if the historian does not bustle in and set them right?[21]

Several recent historians have agreed with Bloch, Carr, Butterfield, and Commager. Richard J. Evans has suggested that historians who use terms such as "wicked" and "evil" in their narratives of the past "will only succeed in looking ridiculous." He says that historians will always be forced to address morally charged issues from the past, but they should engage such issues in their writing and teaching with historical arguments as opposed to "moral or philosophical" ones. Evans uses the case of American slavery as an example. If historians want to show that American slavery was a morally corrupt institution, they should not appeal to the Bible, religious teachings, the conscience, or some other type of moral system. Instead, they should demonstrate, using solid evidence from the past, that slaves suffered, starved, grew sick, and even died as a result of their oppression. He concludes that "overloading the historian's text with expressions of moral outrage will add little to the argument." Most readers and students of history already know that American slavery was a morally reprehensible institution, so why use a book or lesson about slavery to hammer home this point? Instead, historians are required to explain "the attitude

20. Butterfield quoted in Adrian Oldfield, "Moral Judgments in History," *History and Theory* 20, no. 3 (October 1981): 263.
21. Commager, "Should the Historian," 93.

the slaves and slave owners had toward it and why, and what were the larger historical forces behind its rise and fall."[22]

Another modern historian, Brad Gregory (whom we met in chap. 3 and who wrote about his undergraduate experience with Mormonism), argues that the personal moral convictions of historians are "simply and literally irrelevant to understanding the people whom one studies." When historians impose their own beliefs on people or events in the past, they limit their ability to fully understand them. Gregory calls on historians to "bracket" their convictions when interpreting the past. Such bracketing is neither "naïve chimera" nor "impossible." Gregory realizes that casting aside deeply held convictions will be difficult, and he even takes a shot at his fellow historians by suggesting that many of them are "constitutionally incapable" of harnessing their moral opinions, but interpreters of the past should try it nonetheless. "Imperfect self-restraint is better than none."[23] We will return to this idea again in chapters 6 and 7.

Christians may also find the kind of scholarly detachment promoted by Bloch, Carr, Commager, Fischer, Evans, and Gregory to be difficult. As "aliens and strangers" in this world, or those who are "in the world, but not of it," Christians are called to engage in an intellectual practice akin to cultural criticism. To put it differently, Christians should be constantly measuring the spirit of the age over and against the kind of moral practices that define what Jesus called the kingdom of God. When the moral climate of the larger culture fails to conform to the teachings of the Bible or the teachings of the church, Christians must always conform to the values of Scripture and tradition and speak these timeless truths to the world around them. We might disagree on what a Christian cultural critique will look like, but in the end our primary loyalty is to the kingdom of God, not the kingdom of this world.

22. Richard J. Evans, *In Defense of History* (New York: W. W. Norton, 1999), 44.

23. Brad S. Gregory, "The Other Confessional History: On Secular Bias in the Study of Religion," *History and Theory* 45 (December 2006): 147.

If we take seriously the command to "test the spirits to see whether they are from God" (1 John 4:1), then how can we be value free or morally neutral when we are exploring the past and encounter Hitler and the Holocaust, American slavery, Attila the Hun, and other stories and historical actors who, as Christians, we would not hesitate to describe as evil or wicked? If we are to do justice, love kindness, and walk humbly with our God (Mic. 6:8), then we must live prophetically—calling attention to whenever injustice, cruelty, and pride have come to define our society. To paraphrase the activist Howard Zinn, a writer who was never shy about casting moral judgment on the past, "You can't be neutral on a moving train."[24] Similarly, Christians cannot be neutral to the injustices that surround them. They are required to be moral critics.

Steven Keillor, a Christian historian whose work on God's judgments in the past we discussed in the previous chapter, has taken the "Christian historian as moral critic" approach to what appears to be its logical conclusion. In *This Rebellious House: American History and the Truth of Christianity* (a book which Mark Noll describes as "swashbuckling, learned, sometimes infuriating, often surprising, opinionated, pious, devastating, and altogether useful"), Keillor attempts to judge the American past from the perspective of his understanding of Christian orthodoxy.[25] Invoking Ezekiel 2:3, Keillor concludes that the people of the United States, like all humans, have rebelled against God and the very Christian faith that Western civilization has long sought to promote. While the American past has certainly included what Keillor calls "redemptive moments," the overarching theme of the book is that the United States is not a Christian nation but a nation that deserves God's wrath.

Keillor's narrative of American history steers clear of jingoism, patriotism, and triumph. He rails on Columbus and the settlers of

24. Howard Zinn, *You Can't Be Neutral on a Moving Train: A Personal History of Our Times* (Boston: Beacon, 2002).
25. Steven J. Keillor, *This Rebellious House: American History and the Truth of Christianity* (Downers Grove, IL: InterVarsity, 1997); Mark Noll reviews Keillor's book in "American History Through the Eyes of Faith," *Christian Century*, May 21, 1997, 515–18.

the West (Manifest Destiny) for using Christianity to suppress Native American populations. He argues that the United States Constitution is an immoral document for permitting slavery to persist in the new American republic. Americans' long-standing embrace of capitalism has created a nation defined by greed and materialism. Politicians failed to settle their nineteenth-century differences over slavery and states' rights in a civil fashion, choosing instead to embrace pagan notions of honor that ultimately led them into a bloody civil war. Should we call *This Rebellious House* a work of history? It certainly relies on the best historical scholarship and presents one man's interpretation of the past. But Keillor's book is also a work of ethics that applies Christian moral teaching to the actions of people who are dead. Keillor seems to write more like a prophet with a PhD in American history than an evenhanded historian. Yet his work is refreshing, engaging, and has often been celebrated by Christian historians interested in removing the disciplinary boundaries that separate the study of the past from ethical reflection.

While Keillor's interpretation of the past may be a bit "over the top" for some Christian historians, it is not unlike the work of progressive historians (whom we met in chap. 3) who used, and continue to use, the past as a means of pursuing social reform. Can Christian historians balance a moral sensitivity to the injustices of the past with the kind of detachment necessary to fulfill their vocational call to understand the past before judging it? Or should they adopt a Christian version of the approach to the past made popular by twentieth-century progressives? In answering these questions, historian Grant Wacker offers a useful point of departure. He reminds us that historians often serve different roles in society.[26] Historians in the lecture hall or at the seminar table will make sure that their students understand the rules of the academic discipline. They will warn their students about using the past too freely to promote present-day agendas, and they will teach about the importance of historicism—understanding the past on

26. Grant Wacker, "Understanding the Past, Using the Past: Reflections on Two Approaches to History," in Kuklick and Hart, *Religious Advocacy*, 160–66.

its own terms. At other times, historians may be in a position to offer historical information to the public. On these occasions, theory and historiography are often replaced by inspiration or a discussion of the continuity between past and present. And at still other times, historians might write opinion pieces that provide historical perspective on particular issues at stake in public life. Here historians will inevitably make moral judgments, perhaps directing us to a better solution or calling our attention to a road not taken. Historians will have a different agenda speaking to a group of academics at a professional conference than they will in teaching Sunday school. What will remain consistent, however, is the commitment that historians have to understand the past in light of the Five C's discussed in chapter 1.[27]

I recently had the opportunity to hear two lectures—on two consecutive nights—that explored various themes of the past. The first lecture, the annual Messiah College American Democracy Lecture, was presented by Pulitzer Prize–winning historian Annette Gordon-Reed, an expert on Thomas Jefferson and slavery. Gordon-Reed has written extensively on Jefferson's sexual relationship with Sally Hemings, one of the enslaved women on his estate at Monticello, Virginia. Using her expertise as a legal historian, and with the help of DNA evidence, Gordon-Reed argues that Jefferson was the father of all six of Hemings's children.[28] Most early-American historians agree with Gordon-Reed's conclusions, but others, particularly Jefferson's descendants and a few politically conservative writers and groups who want to defend the legacy of our third president and writer of the Declaration of Independence, have rejected her argument.[29]

27. For a useful discussion of the different hats that historians might wear in the course of doing their work, see James M. Banner Jr., *Being a Historian: An Introduction to the Professional World of History* (New York: Cambridge University Press, 2012), especially 158–67.

28. Annette Gordon-Reed, *Thomas Jefferson and Sally Hemings: An American Controversy* (Charlottesville: University of Virginia Press, 1998); *The Hemingses of Monticello: An American Family* (New York: W. W. Norton, 2008).

29. For a critical interpretation of Gordon-Reed's work, but one that has no standing within the community of early-American historians, see David Barton,

While Gordon-Reed delivered a stirring and informative lecture, what caught my attention the most was the level of detachment she applied to her subject. It would have been easy for Gordon-Reed, an African American woman, to use her lecture at Messiah College to cast moral condemnation on Jefferson for his liaison with Hemings and his irresponsible use of the sexual power that he held over her. I later learned that several members of the local African American community, who had come to the lecture hoping to hear Gordon-Reed deliver a condemnatory speech about this incident, were disappointed by her evenhanded explanation of the Jefferson-Hemings affair. Gordon-Reed showed no verbal malice toward Jefferson and did not advocate for Hemings, who was clearly a victim. Instead, speaking as a historian, she presented the case for why she believed Jefferson was indeed the father of the Hemings children and why previous historians have failed to recognize this fact. The morning after the lecture, Gordon-Reed admitted to having personal convictions about the "rightness" or the "wrongness" of Jefferson's behavior but affirmed that as a historian it was not her place to judge Jefferson or use the Jefferson-Hemings affair to preach moral lessons.

The next night, I heard popular writer Eric Metaxas speak about his wildly popular biography of German theologian Dietrich Bonhoeffer. Metaxas's book, *Bonhoeffer: Pastor, Martyr, Prophet, Spy*, has sold thousands of copies to evangelical Christians who want to learn more about the way Bonhoeffer's religious faith inspired him to be a leader in the plot to kill Adolf Hitler, organized by Nazi dissenters in the 1930s and 1940s.[30] Metaxas is a preacher. He employs the past—in this case the heroic story of Bonhoeffer's resistance to Hitler—to inspire the faithful to live better, more Christian lives. During the lecture, he told Bonhoeffer's story in

The Jefferson Lies: Exposing the Myths You've Always Believed About Thomas Jefferson (Nashville: Thomas Nelson, 2012), 1–30. It is worth mentioning that Thomas Nelson ceased publication of *The Jefferson Lies* in August 2012, citing a loss of confidence in the historical accuracy of the book.

30. Eric Metaxas, *Bonhoeffer: Pastor, Martyr, Prophet, Spy* (Nashville: Thomas Nelson, 2010).

a very compelling fashion and then encouraged the audience—mostly evangelicals who had come to Messiah College to hear a sermon—to use Bonhoeffer's life as a model for their Christian journeys in the world. Indeed, as we saw in chapter 2, the past can be useful in our lives as a source of inspiration. I don't know how anyone cannot be inspired by Bonhoeffer's story. I thoroughly enjoyed Metaxas's talk.

Metaxas was using the past in a fundamentally different way than Gordon-Reed did. Metaxas used his subject, Bonhoeffer, as little more than a fifty-minute sermon illustration. Gordon-Reed, however, did not use her subject to preach. While her talk certainly raised a host of moral questions about Jefferson, slavery, race, and so on, and the subject could not help but trigger the moral imagination of the people in the audience, she did not use the Jefferson-Hemings affair as a sermon illustration to inspire us to be strong in the midst of difficult circumstances (as Hemings was in the institution of slavery). She did not use her lecture to rail against the practices of white slaveholders like Jefferson. It would have been easy for her to do this, but she did not. Whatever moral lessons one learned about the past were gleaned through a thorough understanding of the topic rooted in careful and nuanced historical research. I can't help but think that her moral critique was richer and deeper as a result. After listening to both lectures, I realized that I had been given a wonderful teaching moment. Needless to say, the following day I abandoned the syllabus in my historical methods class and took advantage of this opportunity to discuss the meaning of the past and the ways in which it is used in the present.[31]

31. It is worth noting here that Metaxas's book on Bonhoeffer has been harshly criticized by Bonhoeffer scholars who believe that he has presented Bonhoeffer as a sort of twentieth-century evangelical or "born-again" Christian when the evidence seems to suggest that he should be interpreted as a liberal Protestant theologian. See, for example, Richard Weikart's "Metaxas's Counterfeit Bonhoeffer: An Evangelical Critique," www.csustan.edu/history/faculty/weikart/metaxas.htm, accessed November 14, 2012; and Jason B. Hood, "Redeeming Bonhoeffer," *Christianity Today*, February 7, 2011, www.christianitytoday.com/ct/2011/februaryweb-only /redeemingbonhoeffer.html?start=2. Perhaps Metaxas's interest in writing about Bonhoeffer as an inspirational figure for evangelicals (the book is published by

I will close this chapter with five suggestions for those who want to pursue Robert Gleason's idea that the historian should always ask whether or not what happened in the past was "good." First, the historian's *primary* responsibility is explanation and understanding, not moral criticism. In the same way that historians are not responsible for chronicling the special providence of God in human affairs, neither are they predominantly called to give their opinions about the past. Such activity is better left to the ethicists, theologians, and politicians. Those who do want to offer some level of moral reflection on the past should do so only *after* they, their students, and their readers have fully grasped what happened in the past and why it happened in the way it did. Sometimes this kind of moral reflection works better in the classroom than it does in a book, article, or museum exhibit.

Second, when historians do speak or write ethically about what happened in the past, they should do so with caution so that preaching does not trump historical interpretation. In other words, historians should speak *as historians* to the moral concerns of the public. Historians, like everyone else, have opinions, and in the United States they are free to express those opinions, but when speaking to the public *as historians* they must do so with the goal of bringing historical thinking skills to bear on the issue at hand. As historian James Banner has noted, "Reform may arise from historical knowledge, but bringing about reform is the province of others—or at least of historians on their days off."[32]

Third, when a historian engages in moralizing about the past, it should be characterized not only by mature historical understanding but also by mature Christian moral thinking. Indeed, the Bible and church tradition provide Christians with a source of truth that enables us to shed moral light on all of human life, regardless of the era. But for Christian historians to engage in moral criticism well, they must have an adequate theological and biblical understanding

---

evangelical publishing house Thomas Nelson) got in the way of an accurate historical interpretation of Bonhoeffer's life.

32. James Banner Jr., *Being a Historian: An Introduction to the Professional World of History* (New York: Cambridge University Press, 2012), 164.

of the Christian tradition. Sunday school Bible proof-texting will not cut it. Nor will moral platitudes ("Hitler was evil" or "The Declaration of Independence should be praised because it mentions 'God'") that are not grounded in deep theological or ethical thinking. At least one historian has even suggested that historians interested in doing "moral history" should first be trained in the discipline of moral philosophy.[33]

Fourth, historians should make moral judgments in an *implicit* rather than *explicit* manner. Christians who write history should take to heart the words of Adrian Oldfield:

> If the historian litters his account of the past with explicit, stentorian, moral judgments, then the result is likely to be a very ugly piece of historical writing indeed, however much attention he scrupulously pays to evidence. But more judgments do not have to be delivered in such a thunderous manner. Historians can make clear their moral positions implicitly, in terms of the language they use, and in the tone and style of composition.[34]

Historians should also avoid explicit moralizing because we, like the historical actors we write and teach about, are flawed humans. The thoughts about human sin chronicled above should be ever on the mind of Christian historians as they "thunder" their moral and prophetic condemnations on people in the past. As Jesus said, "He who is without sin cast the first stone." George Marsden summarizes it well: "We can point out that we ourselves probably have similar blind spots and that, even though our mistreatment or neglect of our neighbors may not be as notorious or spectacular, we share a common humanity with those whose action we deplore."[35]

Fifth, and finally, historians should also remember to see historical actors as morally complex individuals before casting judgment on them. As mentioned in chapter 1, Jefferson might have been the champion of the ordinary farmer, religious freedom, public

33. John Muresianu, "Toward a New Moral History," *The History Teacher* 17, no. 3 (May 1984): 341.
34. Adrian Oldfield, "Moral Judgments in History," 273.
35. Marsden, "Human Depravity," 32.

education, and small government, but he was also a slaveholder. Or to put this differently, Jefferson owned slaves, but he was also influential in promoting the democratic ideas that eventually led to emancipation. The *complexity* of the past will often trigger our moral imaginations. In a time when our politicians and students rest too comfortably in certitude, history's moral turn may help "create productive confusion and a willingness to recognize that behind all of our moral choices, whether past or present, lurks paradox, tragedy, and irony."[36]

Summing Up

If you are a Christian, I hope that this chapter was useful in helping you to think about the resources within your faith that can help you be a thoughtful student of the past. What if we took the *imago Dei* seriously in our pursuit of history? How might this theological reality shape the history curriculum of a school or college? Rather than teaching courses in non-Western history or the history of American minority groups because we want a diverse curriculum or want to meet certain standards of political correctness, we should try to see through God's eyes the people who have inhabited this world—people with inherent dignity and worth. Of course, it is also important to remember that humans are inherently flawed, and as Matthew 7:1–5 reminds us, we should be very careful about removing the plank from our own eye before we try to remove the speck from the eyes of those whom we encounter in the past. Human sin not only explains why some humans have acted wrongly in the past but also humbles historians who are charged with the task of making sense of such people's lives. A belief in the *imago Dei* and in the sinfulness of humankind can go a long way, as we will see in the next several chapters, toward using the study of the past as a way of working toward a more civil society and a more compassionate Christian faith. And I hope this chapter

36. George Cotkin, "History's Moral Turn," *Journal of the History of Ideas* 69, no. 2 (April 2008): 294.

has at least served as a caution to those who want to condemn the past or use it to teach a moral message. Historians always stir the moral imagination, but they do so implicitly. As storytellers we cannot help but describe things that are "good" and things that are "bad." The human experience is a drama with many ethical twists and turns, but the historian is not always in the business of using his or her voice to preach.

6

History for a Civil Society

O N MARCH 4, 1865, ABRAHAM LINCOLN STOOD BEFORE
the crowd at the United States capitol building to deliver
his second inaugural speech. Lincoln was addressing a nation nearing the conclusion of a long and bloody civil war that
took 750,000 lives. The speech was far from triumphant. It was a
meditation on one of the most tragic moments in American history.
It would have been easy for Lincoln to cast scorn and punishment
down upon the defeated Confederacy. This, after all, is what the
religious leaders of the day had been doing since the outbreak
of war in 1861. Northern ministers believed that the inevitable
Union victory was confirmation that God was indeed on the side
of the North.

But Lincoln wasn't so sure. After all, both sides in this conflict
read the same Bible and prayed to the same God. "The prayers of
both could not be answered; that of neither has been answered
fully. The Almighty has his own purposes," he said. Lincoln would
not settle for easy theological answers. He appealed instead to the
mystery of God. And he made sure that no one in the North would
use the Civil War to bring further division to the country he loved.

Lincoln knew that there were politicians in his own political party who were ready to exploit this tragedy for political gain. These "Radical Republicans" were prepared to humiliate Southerners by making it very difficult for them to return to the Union. With this in mind, Lincoln urged the nation to approach the postwar settlement "with malice toward none, with charity for all." All Americans, Lincoln suggested, were to blame for this ugly war. The hands of both the North and the South had been dirtied by slavery. It was now time for national repentance. Lincoln implied that his Northern politician friends should be careful to take the plank out of their own eye before they passed Reconstruction legislation to remove the speck from the collective eye of the former Confederacy. Invoking Matthew 7:1, he was careful to remind the American people to be cautious about judging the South: "But let us judge not that we be not judged."

Not only was Lincoln charged with the responsibility of bringing the South back into the Union in the wake of the Civil War, but he also was faced with the task of restoring, and then preserving, American democracy amid the culture war—between North and South, Republicans and Democrats—that was on the horizon. He asked the nation to work together in an act of reconciliation to "bind up the nation's wounds; to care for him who shall have borne the battle, and for his widow, and his orphan." Anger and vengeance would do little to promote the kind of civil society necessary for democracy to flourish once again in the United States. To the detriment of the nation, few political leaders took Lincoln's advice. Lincoln would not be alive to see the disastrous culture war that historians refer to as "Reconstruction." It is only in hindsight that we celebrate his famous words.

There are a lot of differences between the country that Lincoln addressed the first week of March 1865 and the country that we live in today. But there are also a lot of similarities. Lincoln knew that our democratic culture would not be sustained by the kind of political and cultural vitriol that he was witnessing in the wake of the Civil War. As we celebrate the 150th anniversary of this tragic event in the American past, democracy is no longer being threatened by secession, slavery, or a bloody civil war, but it is being threatened by our failure to resolve our differences in a civil fashion, work for the common good, and develop the kinds of social virtues necessary for our republic to continue to function. This chapter explores our failure in recent years to live up to the democratic values that we supposedly hold so dear. And it argues that one possible way of invigorating our life together as citizens of the United States is through the study of history.

What Does Democracy Require?

Lincoln was calling us to listen to our better angels. He knew that for a democracy to thrive, citizens needed to learn how to live together with their differences. Today, sociologists, cultural critics, and public intellectuals call the kind of society Lincoln talked about in his second inaugural address a *civil* society. A civil society is one in which citizens foster a sense of community amid their differences. Such a society, as writer Don Eberly describes it, "draws Americans together at a time of social isolation and fragmentation."[1] A successful democracy rests on our ability to forge these kinds of connections and behave in a civil manner toward one another.

A democracy needs citizens—individuals who understand that their own pursuits of happiness must operate in tension with obligations and responsibilities to a larger community. Citizens realize that their own success, fate, and ability to flourish as humans are bound up with the lives of others. Such a commitment to the common good requires citizens who are able to respect, as fellow humans and members of the same community, those with whom they might disagree on some of life's most important issues. It requires empathy, the willingness to imaginatively walk in the shoes of our neighbor.[2] As Mary Ann Glendon puts it, "A democratic

1. Don E. Eberly, "The Meaning, Origins, and Applications of Civil Society," in *The Essential Civil Society Reader: Classic Essays in the American Civil Society Debate*, ed. Don E. Eberly (Lanham, MD: Rowman & Littlefield, 2000), 4.
2. Michael J. Sandel, "Democracy's Discontent: The Procedural Republic," in *Essential Civil Society Reader*, 271; Martha C. Nussbaum, *Not for Profit:*

republic needs an adequate supply of citizens who are skilled in the arts of deliberation, compromise, consensus-building, and reason-giving."[3]

The sixteenth-century writer Montaigne once said, "Every man calls evil what he does not understand."[4] Our everyday lives will always be filled with disagreements and misunderstandings, but a democratic society will survive only if we are able to live civilly with them. We are correct to believe that in the United States we have a "right" to our opinions and beliefs, but there are also times when we must rise above private interests and temporarily sacrifice our rights for the greater good of the larger community. Such a view of the common good, which the late Pope John Paul II called "solidarity," requires that we see others, even those who we may believe are "evil," as neighbors and "sharer[s] on par with ourselves in the banquet of life to which all are equally invited by God."[5] To put an alternative spin on Montaigne's quote, "The more you know about another person's story, the less possible it is to see that person as your enemy."[6]

Because we all have our own views and opinions, civil society requires conversation. We may never come to an agreement on what constitutes the "common good," but we can all commit ourselves to sustaining democracy by talking to and engaging with one another. As author and activist Parker Palmer puts it, "Democracy gives us the right to disagree and is designed to use the energy of creative

Why Democracy Needs the Humanities (Princeton: Princeton University Press, 2010), 6, 7, 10.

3. Mary Ann Glendon, "Rights Talk: The Impoverishment of Political Discourse," in *Essential Civil Society Reader*, 305.

4. Quoted in Joyce Appleby, Lynn Hunt, and Margaret Jacob, *Telling the Truth about History* (New York: W. W. Norton, 1994), 302.

5. Pope John Paul II, *Sollicitudo Rei Socialis*, no. 39, in David J. O'Brien and Thomas Shannon, eds., *Catholic Social Thought: The Documentary Heritage* (Maryknoll, NY: Orbis Books, 1998), 422.

6. Jean Bethke Elshtain, "Democracy on Trial: The Role of Civil Society in Sustaining Democratic Values," in *Essential Civil Society Reader*, 108; Eberly, "The Meaning, Origins, and Applications of Civil Society," in *Essential Civil Society Reader*, 13, 25; Parker J. Palmer, *Healing the Heart of Democracy: The Courage to Create a Politics Worthy of the Human Spirit* (San Francisco: Jossey-Bass, 2011), 5.

conflict to drive positive social change. Partisanship is not a problem. Demonizing the other side is."[7] The inner working of this kind of democracy is described best by the late historian and cultural critic Christopher Lasch in his book *The Revolt of the Elites and the Betrayal of Democracy*. His description of the mechanics of democratic conversation is worth citing in full:

> The attempt to bring others around to our point of view carries the risk, of course, that we may adopt their point of view instead. We have to enter imaginatively into our opponent's arguments, if only for the purpose of refuting them, and we may end up being persuaded by those we sought to persuade. Argument is risky and unpredictable, therefore educational. Most of us tend to think of it . . . as a clash of rival dogmas, a shouting match in which neither side gives any ground. But arguments are not won by shouting down opponents. They are won by changing opponents' minds— something that can only happen if we give opposing arguments a respectful hearing and still persuade their advocates that there is something wrong with those arguments. In the course of this activity, we may well decide that there is something wrong with our own.[8]

Our Current Malaise

Unfortunately, we have failed miserably in sustaining the virtues necessary for a strong democracy. Part of the problem, which sociologists and cultural critics have been decrying for some time, is our rampant selfishness and propensity toward narcissism. Much of what Lasch wrote over thirty-five years ago in his *New York Times* best-selling *The Culture of Narcissism* still rings true today. In fact, the culture of narcissism may have grown even stronger as we enter the twenty-first century. Psychologists Jean Twenge and W. Keith Campbell, writing in 2010, described a "narcissism epidemic," particularly among young people, that has taken the

7. Palmer, *Healing the Heart of Democracy*, 16, 32.
8. Christopher Lasch, *The Revolt of the Elites and the Betrayal of Democracy* (New York: W. W. Norton, 1995), 170–71.

middle-class value of "self-esteem" to a whole new level. They describe an American culture riddled with greed, materialism, and entitlement.[9] Indeed, we live in a culture in which supposed citizens seem to have no obligations or duties to others. The Tea Party movement and other libertarians have convinced millions of Americans that they have to answer to no authority but themselves. Many in our culture have come to define freedom to mean the liberty to do whatever one wants as long as it is within the bounds of the law. In a consumer-driven society, we as individuals have become empowered like never before. The wild growth of capitalism in the United States means that everything is a commodity—something to satisfy our every want and desire. We have been created for something more than this. Yet we continue to deride any quest for the common good as something akin to socialism or anti-Americanism.[10]

Identifying the source of our culture of narcissism would require another book, but part of the problem lies in the way that we educate our children and young adults. During the 2012 Republican presidential primary season, candidate Rick Santorum made news when he called Barack Obama a "snob" for saying that all Americans should get a college education. He supported his attack on the president with the now popular refrain, "College is not for everyone." Some Americans, he said, might be better suited for vocational training, community college, or apprenticeships. It took only a few hours for pundits to figure out that Obama had said basically the same thing in a recent State of the Union address, but in the world of presidential politics, Santorum's remarks probably scored some points among the conservative faithful.

9. Christopher Lasch, *The Culture of Narcissism: American Life in an Age of Diminishing Expectations* (New York: W. W. Norton, 1979); Jean Twenge and W. Keith Campbell, *The Narcissism Epidemic: Living in the Age of Entitlement* (New York: Free Press, 2010).

10. My thoughts here draw on the work of several scholars, including Elshtain, "Democracy on Trial," 107; Charles Mathewes, *The Republic of Grace: Augustinian Thoughts for Dark Times* (Grand Rapids: Eerdmans, 2010), 222; Lasch, *Revolt of the Elites*, 40, 213–14; and Miroslav Volf, *A Public Faith: How Followers of Christ Should Serve the Common Good* (Grand Rapids: Brazos, 2011), 99–100.

But let's consider the position taken by Santorum and Obama on this issue. Were the president and the former senator correct in asserting that a liberal arts education is not for everyone?

Most of our founding founders did not trust the uneducated masses. Many of them believed that common people, because of their lack of education, were not fully equipped for citizenship in a republic. Thomas Jefferson said that a "well-informed citizenry is the only true repository of the public will." When Thomas Paine published *Common Sense*, a 1776 pamphlet that proposed a new American government based on the "common sense" of ordinary people, John Adams called them a "poor, ignorant, malicious, short-sighted, crapulous mass." Jefferson wrote in his *Notes on the State of Virginia* (1782) that "government degenerates when trusted to the rulers of the people alone."[11]

Were the founders right? The debate will continue, but the founders now have some psychological research on their side. David Dunning, a psychologist at Cornell University, and Justin Kruger, a former Cornell graduate student, have found that incompetent people are unable to judge the competence of other people or the validity of their ideas. And their study implies that most people are incompetent. Dunning and Kruger conclude that "very smart ideas are going to be hard for people to adopt, because most people don't have the sophistication to recognize how good an idea is." They add: "To the extent that you are incompetent, you are a worse judge of incompetence in other people." Moreover, Dunning and Kruger have found that most people think too highly of their ability to understand complex ideas. They are self-delusional about their own knowledge. Even when they are judged by an outside evaluator as being poor at a particular task, they claim that their performance was "above average."[12]

If Dunning and Kruger are correct, then what does this say about American democracy? Perhaps the founders were right after all.

11. Thomas Jefferson, *Notes on the State of Virginia*, ed. William Peden (Chapel Hill: University of North Carolina Press, 1982), 148.
12. Natalie Wolchover, "People Aren't Smart Enough for Democracy to Flourish," *Yahoo News*, February 28, 2012.

The founders believed that because people were ignorant by nature, and thus incapable of understanding what was best for the common good, education was absolutely essential to the survival of the American republic. This is why Jefferson founded the University of Virginia, the nation's first public university. This is why George Washington, in his 1796 message to Congress, called for a national university that would teach the arts and sciences. When the founders talked about education, they did not mean vocational training or apprenticeships. While they believed this type of training was certainly important, they also wanted a citizenry trained in government, ethics (moral philosophy), history, rhetoric, science (natural philosophy), mathematics, logic, and classical languages. For these subjects made people informed and civil participants in a democratic society.

I realize that all of this might sound rather elitist. As the product of a working-class family, I have always thought it sounded elitist. Indeed, Santorum and Obama are right when they say that not everyone should get a four-year college education. For our economy to function, we need people who are trained in professional schools, vocational schools, community colleges, and apprenticeships. But is the kind of training necessary for a service-oriented capitalist economy to function the same kind of training necessary for a democracy to flourish? It would seem that the study of literature, philosophy, chemistry, politics, anthropology, biology, religion, rhetoric, economics, and (as we will see below) history is essential for producing the kind of informed citizen, with the necessary virtues and skills, needed for our society to thrive. We have proved that we can educate people for a capitalist economy. We have proved that we can educate people to pursue happiness in a way defined by self-interest, but it appears that we are losing the founders' original vision of education for democracy and the common good.

Instead of engaging in the kind of conversation that is essential to promoting and sustaining a civil society, we have, not unlike bears in the forest, isolated ourselves in our caves only to appear in public spaces—the internet comes immediately to mind—for purposes of roaring in condemnation at those with whom we differ. We can now live in neighborhoods where everyone is just like us. We can get our news from radio and television channels that share our political convictions. (*New York Times* columnist Nicholas Kristof recently described this as our pursuit of the "daily me."[13]) We can attend religious services with people who share our socioeconomic status, skin color, theological beliefs, and style of worship. As Lasch puts it, Americans have "sealed themselves off from arguments and events that might call their own convictions into question, [and] no longer attempt to engage their adversaries in debate." (Unless, of course, it is a five-minute sound bite on cable news shows.) Kristof laments the failure to "work out intellectually with sparring partners whose views we deplore." This is not the behavior of a mature democratic society. How can we take responsibility for our society if we remain in such a state of isolation, growing fat in our ideological enclaves?[14]

History for a Civil Society

Pundits and politicians are full of answers for how to get American democracy on the right track, while others are content with the ongoing cultural wars and see no problem with the virtual collapse of civil society in the United States. I would argue that one small way of cultivating the virtues necessary for a thriving democracy is through the study of history. Let me explain.

I want to begin this section by returning to Stanford education professor and historian Sam Wineburg's masterful work *Historical Thinking and Other Unnatural Acts*. As the country's leading scholar of the teaching of historical thinking skills, Wineburg has argued convincingly that it is the very strangeness of the past that has the best potential to change our lives in positive ways. Those who are willing to acknowledge that the past is a foreign country—a

13. Nicholas Kristof, "The Daily Me," *New York Times*, March 19, 2009.
14. Lasch, *Revolt of the Elites*, 80–81; Elshtain, "Democracy on Trial," 117; Kristof, "Daily Me."

place where they do things differently than we do in the present—set off on a journey that has the potential to transform society.[15] An encounter with the past in all of its fullness, void as much as possible of present-minded agendas, can cultivate virtue in our lives. Such an encounter teaches us empathy, humility, and selflessness. We learn to remove ourselves from our present context in order to encounter the culture and beliefs of a "foreign country." As we saw in chapter 3, sometimes the people who inhabit that country may appear strange when compared with our present sensibilities. Yet the discipline of history requires that we understand them on their own terms, not ours. History demands we set aside our moral condemnation about a person, idea, or event from the past in order to understand it. One cannot underestimate how the virtues learned through historical inquiry also apply to our civic life. The same skills of empathy and understanding that a student or reader of history learns from studying the seemingly bizarre practices of the Aztec Empire might also prove to be useful at work when you don't know what to make of the beliefs or behavior of the person in the cubicle next to yours.

The study of the past has the potential to cure us of our narcissism. The narcissist views the world with himself at the center. While this is a fairly normal way to see the world if you are an infant or toddler, it is actually a very immature way of viewing things if you are an adult. History, to quote Yale historian John Lewis Gaddis, "dethrones" us "from our original position at the center of the universe." It requires us to see ourselves as part of a much larger human story. When we view the world this way, we come face-to-face with our own smallness, our own insignificance.[16] As we begin to see our lives as part of a human community made up of both the living and the dead, we may also start to see our neighbors (and our enemies) in a different light. We may want to listen to their ideas, empathize with them, and try to understand

15. Sam Wineburg, *Historical Thinking and Other Unnatural Acts: Charting the Future of Teaching the Past* (Philadelphia: Temple University Press, 2001), 7.
16. John Lewis Gaddis, *The Landscape of History: How Historians Map the Past* (New York: Oxford University Press, 2002), 4–8.

why they see the world the way they do. We may want to have a conversation (or two) with them. We may learn that even amid our religious or political differences we still have a lot in common.

In their study of popular attitudes toward history, Roy Rosenzweig and David Thelen offer a powerful example of the socially transformative power of engaging with the past. One-sixth of the 1,453 people they polled believed that "an awareness of how people had passed through experiences in the past helped respondents to understand them in the present."[17] These respondents believed that it was equally important to understand the past of a stranger as it was to understand their own. On arriving in New York City, a Jamaican-born immigrant claimed that hearing the stories of how other immigrants arrived in New York before her helped her to humanize them and learn how to live with the city's high level of diversity. Her encounter with people from different cultures and backgrounds led her to conclude that there was a lot in common between her immigration experience and the experiences of her neighbors. As Rosenzweig and Thelen put it, "Understanding the past was a first step toward respecting, and even embracing unfamiliar people, practices, and faiths."[18]

Such an approach to the study of history is summed up best by Wineburg:

> For the narcissist sees the world—both the past and the present—in his own image. Mature historical understanding teaches us to do the opposite: to go beyond our own image, to go beyond our brief life, and to go beyond the fleeting moment in human history into which we have been born. History educates ("leads outward" in the Latin) in the deepest sense. Of the subjects in the secular curriculum, it is the best at teaching those virtues once reserved for theology—humility in the face of our limited ability to know, and awe in the face of the expanse of history.[19]

Are we willing to allow history to "educate" us—to lead us outward?

17. Roy Rosenzweig and David Thelen, *The Presence of the Past: Popular Uses of History in American Life* (New York: Columbia University Press, 1998), 192–93.
18. Ibid.
19. Wineburg, *Historical Thinking*, 24.

Summing Up

As I was working on this book, I was struck by this headline in *USA Today*: "Can the Cause of Social Justice Tame Our Culture Wars?" The piece, written by Tom Krattenmaker, called attention to a group of progressive evangelicals who recently gathered in Portland for a conference devoted to issues facing the next generation of Christian leaders. The event was called the Q Conference, and it focused on the way Christians can be agents of change in the world by working for justice for the poor, abused, enslaved, oppressed, born, unborn, exploited, and mistreated. Krattenmaker suggested that by working together with secularists who are also concerned about social justice, progressive evangelicals could go a long way toward ending the culture wars. I give a hearty amen to the work of the Q Conference and all of those evangelicals concerned with social problems. I have come to know and love a lot of young world-changing evangelicals through my work as a history professor at a Christian college. But after reading Krattenmaker's piece and thinking about how we might end the culture wars, I could not help but wonder if the thing that ails us most is not our failure to engage in activism but our failure to understand and empathize with those with whom we may disagree. Perhaps our failure to bring reconciliation and healing to our divided culture is, at its core, a failure of liberal learning, particularly as it relates to the study of history. Christians and secularists can team up in social justice projects, and Obama can give stirring speeches about ending the Red State–Blue State divide, but until the American people develop the discipline of listening to one another, we will remain stalled in our attempts at reconciliation.

As a Christian, I believe the kind of mutual understanding we need can be accomplished through prayer, hospitality, and Holy Spirit–infused compassion, but it can also be accomplished by training young people to enter worlds—worlds of the past—that are foreign to them. We need to do a better job of teaching young people to interact with the sources and documents from these worlds in a way that requires them to listen and understand before casting judgment. I rarely hear young, progressive, evangelical Christians who want to fight for social justice speak about their callings or vocations in terms of the study of history or some other humanities-related topic. Yet it seems to me that a liberal arts education focused on these disciplines is, without question, the best place to learn the kinds of skills essential to being a world-changer. The study of African history is not going to feed the poor. The study of colonial America will not bring relief to the oppressed. The study of the Russian Revolution is not going to alleviate the plight of the "least of these." But when taught correctly, history will impart the virtues necessary to end the culture wars, transform our ways of thinking about others, and, in some small way, bring meaningful change to the world.

I was recently part of a faculty workshop devoted to spiritual formation. The faculty members participating in the workshop were asked to fill out a questionnaire about the ways we approach our spiritual lives. Based on the results of the questionnaire, the faculty members were placed into one of four "spiritual formation models"—scholar, pietist, contemplative, or activist. I have had moments of deep piety in my life, I am attracted to the contemplative life informed by my childhood Catholicism, and I try to do my part to serve others and be an agent for change in the world, but I fully expected to land in the "scholar" category. I am a productive academic who has written books and articles; I am trying to pursue a life of the mind in the context of my Christian faith. So "scholar" seemed to be a logical fit. Needless to say, I was a bit shocked to learn that my answers to the questionnaire placed me solidly within the "activist" category. I was bothered by this at first. Most of my colleagues in the history department fell safely within the "scholar" category. I thought about this for a few months. I even lost a bit of sleep over it. I was trying to figure out what made me—a fairly traditional historian—an activist. I was not, after all, marching in the streets or active in political campaigns. Yet after much thought about the social virtues that history can cultivate, I have come not only to accept but to embrace the title "historian-activist." I now tell my students that if they want to be world-changers in the present, they need to immerse themselves in the study of the past.

Most of us will think of a historian-activist as someone who tries to use heroic and courageous individuals from the past—people whom we like and whose achievements we celebrate—as a catalyst for social change in the present. But such an approach has its limits. For example, the Southern Poverty Law Center (SPLC) recently did a study showing that schoolchildren are widely ignorant of the civil rights movement. Such a lack of knowledge is problematic, the study argues, because schools that do not adequately teach their students about this great reform movement in American history fail in their responsibility "to educate . . . citizens to be agents of change." The implication is that the study of the past—in this case the study of the heroic leaders of the civil rights movement—will inspire us to go out and do likewise. Indeed, no one will disagree with the notion that the study of heroic individuals in the past can spur us on to great deeds in the present. The past should be inspirational. But how do we use our study of the past to make the world a better place when it does not always inspire us to action? Sometimes—perhaps more often than not—the past is filled with brokenness and sin. It is filled with people whom we may not want our kids to know about. As we have seen, the study of the past always reminds us that we live in a fallen world. Yet we must study it.

Thus, I would argue, we need more than just an awareness of those *courageous* individuals who went before us. We need the kinds of skills the study of the past can inculcate in our lives. The very practice of entering the past—no matter the character of the people we encounter—teaches us social virtues that are essential to making the world a better place. We should be inspiring students toward action by studying the writings of W. E. B. DuBois, Martin Luther King Jr., and Malcolm X, but we should also be instilling them with the kind of empathy for others—even those who seem foreign or strange—that we desperately need in order to "bind up the nation's wounds," heal the culture wars, and, in Lincoln's words, preserve our "last, best hope of earth."

7

The Power to Transform

I N FEBRUARY 2012, PRESIDENT BARACK OBAMA ADDRESSED the National Prayer Breakfast in Washington, DC. He spoke as a Christian. He gave honor and praise to God. He expressed his desire to seek God's face with other Christian believers. He admitted that prayer humbles him. He said that he wakes up every morning and prays, reads the Bible, and has devotions. He noted that his Christian faith motivates him as a leader. He affirmed the words of Jesus: "For everyone to whom much is given . . . much will be required" (Luke 12:48 NKJV). He expressed his belief that the Holy Spirit intervenes in his life, prompting him toward action. He even referenced the time he spent praying with Billy Graham.

It was a powerful speech, but I had a hard time connecting Obama's words with what I heard him say on April 13, 2008. On that evening, I was in Brubaker Auditorium at Messiah College for an event called The Compassion Forum. Obama was joined by Hillary Clinton and the CNN cameras to discuss how faith might inform his policy if he were elected President of the United States. Obama talked about religion as a means by which people get through difficult economic times. He discussed the mystery of

God's will and his inability to fully decipher it. He talked about the need to find ways to reduce abortion. He said he would fight AIDS and poverty around the world.

My failure to harmonize Obama's words at the Prayer Breakfast with his answers to the questions posed to him at The Compassion Forum, and his failure to follow through on those promises while in office, prompted me to devote my weekly column for the religion website Patheos to the problem. In that column, I chided the president for promoting a health care plan that failed to protect the religious freedom of Catholics in regard to contraception. I wrote about how Obama missed a wonderful opportunity to explain his health care proposal—which was disparaged by his Republican rivals as "Obama-care"—as a direct extension of his Christian conviction to care for the poor and needy. And I expressed my disappointment in Obama's failure to keep his promise to reduce abortions in the United States and protect the weakest and most vulnerable of the "least of these."[1]

Very few of the thousands of people who read and commented on my column seemed to realize that it was critical of Obama. That is because about one week after its publication, an article appeared on *The Blaze*, a website affiliated with radio and television pundit Glenn Beck, with the headline: "Messiah College Professor: 'Obama May Be the Most Explicitly Christian President in American History.'"[2] The article itself was an accurate summation of my original Patheos column, but the title that the editors of *The Blaze* chose seized on one particular paragraph that was, at the most, tangential to my larger argument.

I did indeed write that Obama "may be the most explicitly Christian president in American history." I probably should have chosen my words better, but I was trying to argue that there has been no other president in United States history who has used Christian language

1. John Fea, "Would You Vote for This Man?," *Confessing History* (column), February 15, 2012, www.patheos.com/Resources/Additional-Resources/Vote-for -This-Man-John-Fea-02-15-2012.html.

2. Billy Hallowell, "Messiah College Professor: 'Obama May Be the Most Ex-plicitly Christian President in American History,'" *The Blaze*, February 20, 2012, www.theblaze.com/stories/messiah-college-professor-obama-may-be-the-most -explicitly-christian-president-in-american-history/.

to the extent that Obama has. I thought I was on firm ground in this assertion. After all, I had just written an entire book that covered the religious beliefs of the founding fathers.[3] Though these men had lived in an eighteenth-century world in which Christianity was a much more important part of American culture than it is today, they rarely talked about the Bible or Christianity in their public writings and addresses. (George Washington named the name of Jesus Christ only once—and it was just a passing reference!) Any historian writing two hundred years from now and using the same skills of historical investigation that I had used in analyzing the faith of the founders would come to the same conclusion. I was making a historical point, not a political or theological one, although I did imply that I was willing to take Obama at his word when he testified to his Christian faith.

In the midst of our divisive political climate—a culture war in which religion is a prominent battlefield—my article set off a small firestorm. Beck took time on his radio show to attack my credentials as a historian and as a Christian. The article on *The Blaze* received close to nine hundred comments, nearly all of them written by people responding more to the headline than to the substance of my column. The office of human resources at Messiah College received phone calls from Beck fans who wanted me fired. The president of the college fielded angry emails from alumni and donors. The admissions office had to assure some prospective students that we were indeed a Christian college. I received close to one hundred negative emails and telephone messages. Many included nasty expletives. My favorite was a message on my office answering machine from a Beck follower who compared me to Louis Farrakhan, Adolf Hitler, and Woodrow Wilson. (I learned later that these historical figures are popular Beck talking points, but I did not know it at the time.) I responded formally to the attacks only once—in a short blog post called "The Culture Wars Are Real."[4]

3. John Fea, *Was America Founded as a Christian Nation? A Historical Introduction* (Louisville: Westminster John Knox, 2011).
4. John Fea, "The Culture Wars Are Real," *The Way of Improvement Leads Home* (blog), February 21, 2012, www.philipvickersfithian.com/2012/02/culture-wars-are-real.html.

Many of those who left voice mails and sent emails identified themselves as Christians. These were Christians who were ready and willing to call down the wrath of God on me for something I had written that obviously did not conform to their political or religious views. At times I could not tell whether these folks were following Jesus or another messianic figure, namely, Beck. But it was clear to me that Beck's Christian followers—at least the ones whom I had encountered—seemed incapable of engaging with ideas that did not conform to their way of seeing the world, even if those ideas had come from a fellow Christian. In their dogmatism, they had failed—sometimes miserably—to act with a Christlike spirit of love, hospitality, compassion, and understanding for someone whom they perceived to be their political enemy. In the weeks following the response to my column, I thought a lot about how we as believers in Jesus Christ might enter the public sphere with dignity and grace. Much of this thinking has found its way into chapter 6 of this book, but I have also saved some of it for this chapter. I argue, with the help of several political theologians, that our failure to participate in public debate with a degree of civility and understanding not only damages the witness of the church in the world, but it impoverishes our spiritual lives. Or to put it in a more positive light: an encounter with people of different beliefs may not only contribute to a civil society but also help us grow as Christians.

So what does this have to do with history? The study of the past, while it is certainly no replacement for the power of the Holy Spirit in our lives and communities, can make a modest contribution to our spiritual formation. This chapter offers Christians an approach to thinking about the past that avoids the danger of present-mindedness, the certainty of providentialism, and the temptation to trade history for moral criticism. While this approach is grounded in the idea that all of the past is important because it is the ongoing work of God's creation, it offers a more practical benefit for Christians and intersects with some of the best and most recent scholarship in historical thinking. My argument is this: the study of history can help Christians mature spiritually by teaching us to love God and love our neighbor.

Any first-year history student who takes one of my courses will quickly learn the name Sam Wineburg. When I first read his book *Historical Thinking and Other Unnatural Acts*, it changed the way I think about the past and how I teach future teachers to teach history. I have recommended this book to hundreds of schoolteachers during professional development seminars I conduct around the country. If you have read this far, you know that there is much about Wineburg's book that has inspired what I have written here. With this in mind, I want to once again quote from what I believe to be the most important and inspirational paragraph in Wineburg's book. It is a quote currently posted on my office door and has come to be a sort of mission statement for what I do as a historian and college history teacher.

> For the narcissist sees the world—both the past and the present—in his own image. Mature historical understanding teaches us to do the opposite: to go beyond our own image, to go beyond our brief life, and to go beyond the fleeting moment in human history into which we have been born. History educates ("leads outward" in the Latin) in the deepest sense. Of the subjects in the secular curriculum, it is the best at teaching those virtues once reserved for theology—humility in the face of our limited ability to know, and awe in the face of the expanse of history.[5]

Wineburg's words here are similar, and perhaps even draw upon, a remark on the teaching of history by University of Pennsylvania historian Walter A. McDougall:

> If honestly taught, history is the only academic subject that inspires humility. Theology used to do that, but in our present era—and in public schools especially—history must do the work of theology. It is, for all practical purposes, the religion of the modern curriculum. Students whose history teachers discharge their intellectual and civic responsibilities will acquire a sense of the contingency of all human endeavor, the gaping disparity between motives and

5. Sam Wineburg, *Historical Thinking and Other Unnatural Acts: Charting the Future of Teaching the Past* (Philadelphia: Temple University Press, 2001), 24.

consequences in all human action, and how little control human beings have over their own lives and those of others. A course in history ought to teach wisdom—and if it doesn't, then it is not history but something else.[6]

In this chapter I want to focus on both Wineburg's and McDougall's reference to the relationship between history and theology, and history's ability to transform our behavior.

History as Public Engagement

As we saw in the previous chapter, Americans live in isolated enclaves that make it difficult for them to engage in public with people who are not like them. American Christians are also guilty of this kind of isolationism. God wants us to turn toward him, but he also wants us to turn toward others in a spirit of Christian love and understanding. Yet it is much easier to escape to the comfortable enclaves we have created for ourselves where everyone is just like us. Such cultural isolationism prevents us from getting to know people who represent a different political orientation, religious belief, class, race, or sexual orientation. Or perhaps our escapism is more theological in nature—a belief that human history has already been "scripted" by God. Such an eschatological approach to life teaches us that this world is not as important as the next one, so we do not need to invest in it with any degree of seriousness. According to theologian Charles Mathewes, this kind of escapism weakens our spiritual lives, for public engagement cultivates Christian character, purifies our souls, and prepares us for our heavenly home. In the process of loving our neighbor—a practice that goes to the heart of civic life—we grow as Christians.[7]

6. Walter A. McDougall, "Teaching American History," *The American Scholar* (Winter 1998): 102.
7. Charles Mathewes, "Author Meets His Critics: 'A Theology of Public Life,' Opening Remarks" (panel, Boisi Center for Religion and American Public Life, Boston College, Chestnut Hill, Massachusetts, October 11, 2007), http://frontrow .bc.edu/program/mathewes/; Mathewes, *The Republic of Grace: Augustinian Thoughts for Dark Times* (Grand Rapids: Eerdmans, 2010), 11, 38, 202–3.

Humans need to live in society. We fulfill our vocations as Christians in the world through dialogue with and service to others. It is the place where we work out our salvation and exercise our spiritual gifts and talents.

What if we viewed the study of the past as a form of public engagement? Like any type of public engagement, an encounter with the strangeness of the past can inevitably lead, in Mathewes's words, "to contemplation of the mysteries of providence, the sovereignty of God, and the cultivation of the holy terror that is integral to true piety."[8] Even if the people we engage with are dead, we can still enter into a conversation with the sources that they have left behind. In a passage strikingly familiar to Wineburg's and McDougall's thoughts on the discipline of history, Mathewes argues that when we encounter people in all their strangeness we

> find ourselves decentered, we find that we are no longer the main object of our purposes, but participate in something not primarily our own. This confession then is itself a turning to the other, not in the interests of mutual narcissism—which makes the other only a consolation prize for having to be already ourselves—but as an openness to transforming, and being transformed by, the other.[9]

If we take the *imago Dei*—the notion that all humans are created in the image of God—seriously, then we should also take seriously the idea that those who lived in the past were also created in God's image. The very act of studying humanity—past or present—can be a means by which we experience God. The study of the past thus becomes an act of spiritual devotion than can provide "more than enough opportunities for humility and penance, recognition of one's sin and the sins of others, and a deepening appreciation of the terrible awe-fulness of God's providential governing of the world."[10]

8. Mathewes, *Republic of Grace,* 242.
9. Ibid., 210.
10. Mathewes, *A Theology of Public Life* (New York: Cambridge University Press, 2007), 166.

History as Love

Love is at the center of the Christian life. It is one of the "fruits of the Spirit" recorded in Galatians 5:22–23. Jesus reminded us that "greater love has no one than this: to lay down one's life for one's friends" (John 15:13). His sacrificial death on the cross exemplified the ultimate act of love (Phil. 2:6–8). In the Christian tradition, we flourish as human beings when we learn to live the "Jesus Creed"—loving the Lord our God with all our heart, mind, soul, and strength, and loving our neighbor as ourselves. Such sacrificial love for God and neighbor is the source of true joy and happiness. In the words of St. Paul, "I have been crucified with Christ and I no longer live, but Christ lives in me. The life I now live in the body, I live by faith in the Son of God, who loved me and gave himself for me" (Gal. 2:20). As theologian Miroslav Volf reminds us, "At the core of the Christian faith lies the persuasion that . . . 'others' need not be perceived as innocent in order to be loved, but ought to be embraced even when they are perceived as wrongdoers. . . . The story of the cross is about God who desires to embrace precisely the 'sons, and daughters of hell.'" Our lives should be one of "embrace" rather than "exclusion."[11]

The study of the past offers endless opportunities to exercise loving embrace to our fellow humans, even if they have lived in a different era and are no longer alive. It is easy to manipulate the voices from the past to serve our own purposes in the present, and out of love we must not do this. As we saw in chapter 3, this kind of presentism makes for bad history, and when looked at theologically, this kind of manipulation is also a failure to love—a failure to enter into the worlds of those who have gone before us with a spirit of compassion, selflessness, and empathy. (Such a failure to love God and others is the equivalent of sin.) People in the past cannot

11. Miroslav Volf, *A Public Faith: How Followers of Christ Should Serve the Common Good* (Grand Rapids: Brazos, 2011), 70–72; Scot McKnight, *The Jesus Creed: Loving God, Loving Others* (Brewster, MA: Paraclete Press, 2004); Volf, *Exclusion and Embrace: A Theological Exploration of Identity, Otherness, and Reconciliation* (Nashville: Abingdon, 1996), 69–71, 85.

defend themselves. They are at the mercy of the historian. This, of course, gives the practitioner of history a great deal of power. But Christian historians will do their best to meet the people in the past as Jesus encountered the people he met during his earthly ministry. They must relinquish power and avoid the temptation to use the powerless—those in the past who are at the mercy of us, the interpreters—to serve selfish ends, whether they be religious, political, or cultural. The exercise of this hermeneutic of love means that we will read historical texts for the purpose of learning how to love people who are not like us, perhaps even people who, if we were living at the same time, may have been our enemies.[12] It forces us to love others—even a nineteenth-century slaveholder or Hitler—when they seem to be unlovable. Failure to respect the people in the past is ultimately a failure of love. It is a failure to recognize the common bond that we share with humanity.

When a historian interprets the past, he or she participates in the act of welcoming strangers. Historians should be in the business of practicing hospitality, and in the Christian tradition "hospitality" and "exclusion" are incompatible terms.[13] Doing history will require "intellectual hospitality," or the willingness to engage the ideas of people from the past with humility. Such intellectual hospitality requires us to approach a primary source with a mindset that the author of such a text knows more about the particular subject than we do and can thus serve as a guide toward a full understanding of what it has meant to be human.[14] The exercise of showing intellectual hospitality to the dead is not easy. It does not come naturally. But like all good history, such an act of compassion and love for those in the past requires imagination and an openness to listen before judging.

12. Beth Barton Schweiger, "Seeing Things: Knowledge and Love in History," in *Confessing History: Explorations in Christian Faith and the Historian's Vocation*, ed. John Fea, Jay Green, and Eric Miller (Notre Dame, IN: University of Notre Dame Press), 60–82.

13. Christine D. Pohl, *Making Room: Recovering Hospitality as a Christian Tradition* (Grand Rapids: Eerdmans, 1999), 31.

14. Kim S. Phipps, "Campus Climate and Christian Scholarship," in *Scholarship and Christian Faith: Enlarging the Conversation*, ed. Douglas Jacobsen and Rhonda Hustedt Jacobsen (New York: Oxford University Press, 2004), 174.

Such an approach to Christian hospitality might also have implications for the way we teach about the past. I think we need to get into the habit of establishing ground rules of hospitality in our classrooms. Such ground rules should be instituted on the first day and enforced diligently. It is important that a teacher develop a classroom culture of respect. Such respect should flow not only from student to teacher (and vice versa) and student to student but also from student to the historical subject under consideration. In other words, we need to show respect to the dead. While this may sound strange, or even a bit eerie, respect for the dead is essential if the kind of historical learning I have described above is going to take place.[15]

If a given history classroom has twenty students, and the teacher is the twenty-first member of the class, we should remind our students that there is also a twenty-second person "in the room," namely, the author of the primary document under consideration on that particular day. The author of that document deserves the same kind of respect that a teacher deserves and that each student deserves. In my classroom, I will not allow students to say anything (negative or positive) about a particular document until they have first "listened" to what the author is trying to say. As we saw in chapter 3, our "psychological condition at rest" leads us to judge someone from the past, but historical thinking is an "unnatural act." The twenty-second person "in the room" should be treated with Christian love. He or she must be welcomed as a stranger. This is the essence of intellectual hospitality. In the case of a school or college classroom, such hospitality is cultivated by habit. In the process, students not only learn to be better historical thinkers, but they also learn transferable lessons about how to live Christianly in this world.

History as a Spiritual Discipline

When looked at this way, history is not only a discipline in the academic sense in which philosophy or literary criticism or sociology

15. On respect for the dead, see Jonathan Gorman, "Historians and Their Duties," *History and Theory* 43, no. 4 (December 2004): 115.

are disciplines. It is also a discipline in the sense that it requires patterns of behavior, such as the denial of self, that are necessary in order to meet the "other" in a hospitable way. Doing history is not unlike the kind of "disciplines" we employ in our spiritual lives—disciplines that take the focus off of us and put it on God or others. As historian Beth Barton Schweiger writes, "The discipline of history can be a means of grace in the life of the historian. The writing of history, rightly done, can challenge and change the historian."[16] For generations, historians have seen the pursuit of objectivity—the need to cast aside personal bias in order to tell a story about the past that is as accurate as possible—as an effort of the will.[17] Historian Thomas Haskell, a noted authority on the subject of historical interpretation, writes,

> The very possibility of historical scholarship as an enterprise distinct from propaganda requires of its practitioners that vital minimum of ascetic discipline that enables a person to do such things as abandon wishful thinking, assimilate bad news, discard pleasing interpretations that cannot pass elementary tests of evidence and logic, and, most important of all, suspend or bracket one's own perceptions long enough to enter sympathetically into the alien and possibly repugnant perspectives of rival thinkers. . . . Fairness and honesty are qualities we can rightfully demand of human beings, and those qualities require a very substantial measure of self-overcoming. . . . Objectivity is not something entirely distinct from detachment, fairness, and honesty, but is the product of extending and elaborating these priceless and fundamentally ascetic virtues.[18]

While Christian historians need willpower as well, we can also rely on prayer, the Holy Spirit's power, and other spiritual practices in order to pursue the kind of self-denial, hospitality, charity, and humility needed to engage the past in a proper way and be open to

---

16. Schweiger, "Seeing Things," 63.

17. Peter Novick, *That Noble Dream: The "Objectivity Question" and the American Historical Profession* (New York: Cambridge University Press, 1988), 101.

18. Thomas L. Haskell, *Objectivity Is Not Neutrality: Explanatory Schemes in History* (Baltimore: Johns Hopkins University Press, 1998), 148–49. I am thankful to L. D. Burnett for bringing this quotation to my attention.

the possibility of its transforming us. How often do we pray over our scholarly historical work? And I don't mean a prayer for help in getting the paper done on time or a prayer that we keep our sanity amid the heavy workload. I mean a prayer that the Lord would use our study of the past in all its fullness to change us. Similarly, when we uncover sinful behavior in the past, it should cause us to examine our own imperfect lives. It might even lead to prayers of confession. When we are open to using the past as a mirror that forces us to come to grips with our own flaws, we relieve ourselves of the "humanly inescapable desire to judge, and ultimately to *be* the judge, to be the author of our own story, to be God."[19] The practice of confession draws us closer to God and others, but it also enables us to be more effective historians—scholars and students who are better able to understand and tell the stories of people who live in the "foreign country" of the past.

I have posted above my desk (in the office where I do most of my historical work) a "prayer before study" written by the Catholic scholastic Thomas Aquinas. Though I am not always as consistent as I would like to be, I try to pray it whenever I sit down to write or conduct research into the past. I have even brought it with me when I visit archives. Though the prayer is not specifically geared toward historians, I often make adaptations to fit the particular historical task at hand. Praying this prayer settles me in my work and decenters me. It is a reminder that God is with me, helping me to get out of the way so that I can listen more attentively to the voices from the past that I will be encountering that day.

Thomas Aquinas, "A Prayer before Study"

Ineffable Creator,
Who, from the treasures of Your wisdom,
has established three hierarchies of angels,
has arrayed them in marvelous order
above the fiery heavens,
and has marshaled the regions

19. Mathewes, *Republic of Grace*, 211.

of the universe with such artful skill,
You are proclaimed
the true font of light and wisdom,
and the primal origin
raised high beyond all things.
Pour forth a ray of Your brightness
into the darkened places of my mind;
disperse from my soul
the twofold darkness
into which I was born:
sin and ignorance.
You make eloquent the tongues of infants.
Refine my speech
and pour forth upon my lips
the goodness of Your blessing.
Grant to me
keenness of mind,
capacity to remember,
skill in learning,
subtlety to interpret,
and eloquence in speech.
May You
Guide the beginning of my work,
direct its progress,
and bring it to completion.
You Who are true God and true Man,
Who live and reign, world without end.
Amen.[20]

When we see our work as historians as a spiritual exercise, we also find that we grow in wisdom. An encounter with the strangeness and diversity of the past, or even a part of the past that we might find familiar, will force us to come to grips with new ways of thinking and looking at the world. This kind of encounter, as Mathewes describes it in the context of civic engagement in

20. Thomas Aquinas, "A Prayer Before Study," in *Raccolta #764, Pius XI Studiorum Ducem*, 1923, adapted by Jeff Barneson, July 2, 2004, www.intervarsity.org/slj/article/2442.

contemporary life, "brings us repeatedly against the stubborn, bare there-ness of the people we meet in public life; it teaches us again and again the terrible lesson that there are other people, other ideals, other points of view that we can see and appreciate, even if we cannot inhabit them and remain ourselves."[21] We do not have to agree with every idea we encounter in the past. Sometimes we cannot "inhabit" an idea and still "remain ourselves." But education—to be led outward—does require a degree of risk. As historian and educator Mark Schwehn writes, we must "be willing to give up what we think we know for what is true." Without taking a risk, without being open to transformation, genuine education cannot happen. A history education, like education in most of the humanities-based disciplines, can be painful because it requires self-denial and a "willingness to surrender ourselves for the sake of a better opinion." But wisdom "is the discernment of when it is reasonable to do so."[22]

I often tell my students that when their study of the past exposes them to a new way of thinking, they need to grapple intellectually with such an idea to the point of losing sleep. (After all, college students don't sleep, right?) They need to discern whether or not they can incorporate this new idea into their way of viewing the world. Or perhaps they need to change their way of viewing the world in order to accommodate an idea that they believe to be true. This kind of wisdom requires prayer and spiritual discipline. It also requires community. This might mean conversations—with roommates, friends, classmates, family, professors, and pastors—about whether the idea is worthy of embrace. Christians who study the past must be prudent. They must be slow to speak and quick to listen to the people they meet in the past. And they must seek wisdom.

I will end this chapter with the stories of two former students who have experienced the transformative experience of doing history. I will begin with Kelly. A couple of years ago, Kelly was hard at work on her senior thesis—a study of the Baptist preacher and

21. Mathewes, *Republic of Grace*, 304.
22. Mark Schwehn, *Exiles from Eden: Religion and the Academic Vocation in America* (New York: Oxford University Press, 1993), 49.

political activist Jerry Falwell and the rise of the Christian Right. At first glance, one might find Kelly's topic to be typical for a student at a Christian college. Many students who arrive at Christian liberal arts colleges have been shaped, in one way or another, by political and evangelical conservatism. I honestly don't know if Kelly had an experience in her childhood with the Christian Right, but if she did, she had long abandoned such commitments. During her years on campus, she was very active in liberal causes and served as a local organizer for Obama's presidential run in 2008. In fact, I can think of only a handful of students I have taught who shared Kelly's commitment to liberal politics. (I can also think of only a handful of students who shared Kelly's passion for history.) So when I heard about the subject of Kelly's senior thesis (it was supervised by a colleague), I was concerned. I thought that there was a good chance she would use her project to do a hatchet-job on Falwell and the Christian Right. My concern had nothing to do with politics and everything to do with history. Could Kelly write a historical study of this movement and its founder without allowing her political convictions, which were diametrically opposed to the views of her subject, to limit her historical understanding?

As usual, Kelly was up to the challenge. As we talked about the work she was doing on her thesis—which included both archival research and oral history—it was clear that Kelly had made a conscious decision to treat Falwell and the rise of a Christian Right as a historian and not as a political junkie. But it was not easy. Kelly was forced to spend hundreds of hours reading sources that grated on her own political beliefs. My conversations with her, and her regular Facebook updates to friends, revealed that she was engaged in one of the toughest intellectual exercises of her life. The challenge was less about collecting data and synthesizing it into a well-written paper. She had done this many times before and was quite good at it. No, the real challenge was trying to empathize with a historical figure and movement with which she had fundamental disagreements.

Kelly found that it was her deep and abiding Christian faith that helped carry her through her historical work. She found in Jesus's life and commands a model of love that was self-sacrificial and even self-abasing in character. And she saw the necessity to apply this to her academic pursuits. Kelly had to put her own opinions and impressions aside and portray Falwell as a complex person reacting to events that she did not experience. She knew that her own feelings and experiences stood in the way of this kind of assessment. She asked God to forgive her for the hatred that she let live in her heart and for the condemnatory attitude with which she was approaching her research. She asked God to turn the weakness inherent in her lack of historical empathy into strength. Kelly had no choice but to cultivate an intellectual dependency on Christ, and she felt his presence as she completed her project, doing her best to resist the "prejudices, myopic interpretations, and lack of compassion that so easily ensnared." She was aware that historians cannot avoid some degree of bias. But as Kelly put it, "Bias is one thing; outright acrimony is another."

I am happy to report that Kelly delivered an outstanding senior thesis. She proved to everyone in attendance at her defense that she has a promising career as a historian ahead of her. She also matured in the process. On a few occasions, Kelly went beyond empathy for her subject to exercise a degree of sympathy. While her political convictions did not change one iota during the project, she found herself, toward the end of her writing, defending Falwell against his critics who did not fully understand him and his motivations or who were treating him unfairly. In the process, Kelly learned to love her neighbor.[23]

In my second concluding story, I return to my discussion in chapter 3 regarding teaching texts written by nineteenth-century pro-slavery intellectuals. Just like everyone else in my class, Kevin was appalled at the arguments contained in these documents. But by entering into a conversation with their authors and being open to letting these writers change him, he became a better Christian. Let me explain. Kevin learned that plantation owners often argued

23. This account is based partly on an email exchange with "Kelly." I have included some quotations from that email, but most of what I have written is a paraphrase of what she wrote to me.

that slavery was justified because slaveholders treated their labor force (slaves) better than the burgeoning capitalists of the North treated their immigrant laboring class. Slaves were clothed, fed, and Christianized and usually worked ten hours a day. Northern industrial laborers (living in an age with none of the benefits afforded to workers today) worked sixteen-hour days, were paid so poorly that they could not provide the basics for their families, and generally lived lives that were much worse than those of Southern slaves. *How dare the Northern abolitionists and capitalists claim the moral high ground,* Kevin thought. *How dare they accuse slaveholders of immorality while all the while turning a blind eye to the plight of the working-class "slaves" in their midst!* The South's anticapitalist feudalism offered, as historians Elizabeth Fox-Genovese and Eugene Genovese have shown, one of the most powerful critiques of industrialization in nineteenth-century America.[24] Kevin was swayed by the argument.

But Kevin was also convinced that the slaveholders' criticism of Northern industry did not get them off the moral hook. Slavery was still a reprehensible and sinful practice, and Kevin was not sure that this defense of slavery was valid. The Northern workers may have had it rough, perhaps even rougher than slaves, but at least they were free. Kevin did, however, learn to be cautious about condemning others before hearing their side of the story. His response to these writers was not a knee-jerk moral criticism but a thoughtful engagement with historical texts that taught him a valuable lesson about removing the log from your own eye before taking the speck out of the eye of another. Kevin listened to the slaveholders. He understood them. He empathized with them. He saw them as fellow humans. He realized that some of their flaws were also present in his own life and his relationships with others. And in the process he was, in a small way, changed. At the end of the course, he told me that his close reading of the slaveholder documents had made him a more compassionate and understanding

24. Elizabeth Fox-Genovese and Eugene Genovese, *The Mind of the Master Class: History and Faith in the Southern Slaveholders' Worldview* (New York: Cambridge University Press, 2005).

person when encountering those with whom he did not agree. He would look for opportunities to empathize with his enemies—even love them—before condemning them. Are not these the kinds of transformative encounters that we want students of the past to experience? It seems likely that dozens and dozens of such encounters would add up to make someone a mature individual, an informed citizen, and a better Christian.[25]

I wish I could say that Kelly and Kevin represent the way most of us approach historical texts, but that is not the case. However, Kelly and Kevin demonstrate that real transformation is possible when we are exposed to opinions that we naturally find uncomfortable. History students do not have to agree with slaveholders to learn something from them, even if it is only to remind themselves that they, like the authors of these texts, are imperfect creatures in need of improvement and redemption. This is what history can do, and this is why Christians must study it. We need to study history not because it can win us political points or help us push our social and cultural agendas forward, but because it has the amazing potential to transform our lives.

25. Kevin is a pseudonym for a student in my "United States History to 1865" course at Messiah College, Fall 2006.

8

So What Can You Do with a History Major?

ARA IS A FORMER STUDENT OF MINE. SHE WAS AN UN-
dergraduate history major who now works at a children's
hospital in the Republic of Malawi in southern Africa. Her
job consists of spending time with sick children. She plays with
them, builds relationships with them and their parents, listens to
them, empathizes with their struggles, and then tells their stories
to Western Christians through a variety of social media outlets.
To borrow a phrase from James Davison Hunter's *To Change the
World*, Tara is "faithfully present" in the lives of these Malawian
children and their families. She is devoting her life to something
greater than her own ambitions. She is an agent of change in the
world. And she got this job *because* and not *in spite* of the fact
that she was a history major in college.

Tara landed this job because she writes well, listens well, and
is a good storyteller. Isn't this what historians do? They listen to
people (in Tara's case, the children in the hospital), interpret what
they have heard, and communicate their stories to a larger audience.

These skills, which Tara was able to articulate in her job interview, would have been enough to make her an impressive candidate for this kind of work. But Tara was also able to explain the ways in which her study of history has cultivated virtues in her life that are necessary to engage a world that is different from her own. As a student of history, she learned to listen to voices from the past, to walk in the shoes of others (even if they were dead), and to step outside her own moment in time and her own self-interested approach to the world and try to understand the hopes, dreams, struggles, and mindsets of people who were from another era or who held beliefs that did not conform to her own. In this sense, the study of history humanized her. Tara knows that history can help us to be reconcilers and humble servants to those in need.

Needless to say, I am proud of Tara. She has used the skills and virtues she gained as a historian to forge a meaningful vocation. I don't know how long she will stay in Malawi, but wherever she goes, the things she has learned as a historian will enable her to find work and to live a life of empathy, service, and love. Tara is not alone. For the past several years I have been writing a regular series at my blog, titled "So What CAN You Do with a History Major?" Through this series, I have heard from dozens of people who are using their history majors in creative ways. History professors and teachers from around the country email to tell me how the series has been useful to them and their students. My goal with this series was to focus my attention on people who studied history in college but did not pursue a career in a history-related field. I was not interested in hearing from history teachers and professors, public historians and preservationists, or graduate students in history. Instead, I wanted to hear the stories of those who have pursued careers in other fields but who, if they had to do it again, would still study history because the skills they learned have been useful to their current vocations.

There are a lot of history majors out there. Some of them are famous. It only takes a quick internet search to find successful people who studied history in college. Though I have no idea if these people find the skills they learned as students of history to be useful in their current professions, it is worth mentioning their names, if only to encourage college history majors (and their parents) that those who study the past have gone on to do important and worthwhile things. The list includes George W. Bush (president of the United States), Franklin D. Roosevelt (president of the United States), Antonin Scalia (Supreme Court justice), Martha Stewart (entertainer), Katharine Hepburn (actor), Bill Bradley (United States senator and presidential candidate), Kareem Abdul-Jabbar (NBA player), Ralph Winter (movie producer of *X-Men* and *The Fantastic Four*), Wolf Blitzer (CNN anchor), Steve Carell (actor), Bill O'Reilly (news pundit), Richard Nixon (president of the United States), Sam Palmisano (CEO of IBM), Theodore Roosevelt (president of the United States), Will Forte (actor and comedian), Newt Gingrich (speaker of the House of Representatives), Jackie Joyner-Kersee (Olympic athlete), Julia Child (chef), George McGovern (United States senator and presidential candidate), Grant Hill (NBA player), Chelsea Clinton (daughter of Bill and Hillary Clinton and hedge-fund manager), Sonia Sotomayor (Supreme Court justice), Pat Robertson (televangelist), Joe Biden (vice president of the United States), Charlie Rose (journalist), Larry David (coproducer of *Seinfeld*), Gordon Brown (prime minister of the United Kingdom), Orrin Hatch (United States senator), Sacha Baron Cohen (comedian and actor), Stockard Channing (actor), Chris Berman (ESPN sports broadcaster), Charles Kuralt (newsman), Jimmy Buffett (singer-songwriter), Conan O'Brien (talk-show host and comedy writer), Adlai Stevenson (governor of Illinois and presidential candidate), W. E. B. DuBois (cofounder of the NAACP), Christa McAuliffe (teacher who died in the space shuttle *Challenger*), and Carly Fiorina (CEO of Hewlett-Packard).[1]

These famous history majors reinforce a statistic from Philip Gardner, a career specialist at Michigan State University: 40 percent of employers today do not care about a student's major. All

1. John Fea, "So What CAN You Do with a History Major?—Part 4," *The Way of Improvement Leads Home* (blog), December 8, 2009, www.philipvickers fithian.com/2009/12/famous-history-majors.html.

of these men and women must have enjoyed the study of the past (after all, they stuck with it for four years in college), but none of them became professional historians.[2]

If you are reading this book, there is a good chance that you are either a student of history or a teacher of history. I hope that the stories of the more ordinary students of history that I have assembled below will inform and inspire you to think about the ways that you can make your study of the past work for you as you pursue a variety of vocations and jobs in our ever-changing marketplace.

So What Can You Do with a History Major?

Work for Social Justice in the World

Jeff was a public history student in college. He now works for AmeriCorps VISTA, a national service program designed to fight poverty in the United States. With a history degree, Jeff thought he would pursue a career in a museum or historical society until he met a friend who had returned from service in the Peace Corps. His friend told him about AmeriCorps, and Jeff saw work in this agency as an excellent way to use his love of history and community building in a "job that paid." He was assigned to the Center for Art and Community Partnerships at the Massachusetts College of Art (MassArt) in Boston. His job is to build relationships between MassArt and its neighboring communities through discussions about how "art and history can catalyze and promote social change." As a historian, he knows how history "connects people, places, and things to communities." He is an effective communicator and understood the importance of critical thinking to his work in these neighborhoods. As Jeff puts it, "Much of public history started as people's history, which served and celebrated an important democratic function of giving

2. Philip D. Gardner, panelist for "Employment and Market Data and Trends" (Rethinking Success Conference, Wake Forest University, April 11, 2012), www.youtube.com/watch?v=ILMhDgWtNsA&feature=youtu.be.

[local communities the rights] and resources to chronicle and tell their own history."[3]

Become a Writer

Sonia is a Pulitzer Prize–winning reporter and bestselling author who has spent twenty years reporting and writing about social issues for one of the largest metropolitan newspapers in the country. Her stories have tackled some of this country's most intractable problems: hunger, drug addiction, immigration. She has been named among the most influential Latinos by *Hispanic Business Magazine* and a "trendsetter" by *Hispanic Magazine*. Sonia majored in history at a liberal arts college in the Northeast and later pursued a master's degree in Latin American studies. She believes that a history major is the best foundation for a career in journalism. Her studies in history helped her to do research, taught her where to look for needed documents, and made her a better writer. She adds, "More important, however, [my history major] taught me to think critically. Because when you look at events in history, by looking at how those situations were resolved you can understand a lot about what is going to happen in the future. The past is prologue." Sonia believes that employers are always looking for people who can do research, think critically, place current events in historical context, and write clearly. She concludes that she "cannot think of a better major that gives you all that."[4]

Tony is also a Pulitzer Prize–winning journalist and author. A native of Washington, DC, he holds an undergraduate degree in history and a graduate degree in journalism. He has been a staff writer and international correspondent for two major New York newspapers. Tony never planned to be a journalist when he enrolled in college, but studying history taught him how to view sources

3. Jeff Robinson, "An Alternative Space for Public History: AmeriCorps," *History@Work*, April 24, 2012, publichistorycommons.org/an-alternative-space-for-public-history-americorps/.

4. John Fea, "So What CAN You Do with a History Major?—Part 25," *The Way of Improvement Leads Home* (blog), March 23, 2010, www.philipvickersfithian.com/2010/03/so-what-can-you-do-with-history-major.html.

critically and skeptically. As a history major, he learned to distill vast amounts of information into a concise story or argument. He learned the importance of context. Tony advises students of history not to sweat the names and dates. "You'll forget all the substance five years out, but hopefully retain a few of the skills. It's a cliché, I know, but school is mainly about learning how to learn so you can keep educating yourself once you're out. I regard my so-called career, first as a journalist and now as book author, as continuing education, without the tests and grades and tuition."[5]

Work in the Field of Marketing and Communications

Several summers ago, Cali, a college history major, accepted a full-time summer position as the marketing and communications associate at a boutique asset management firm in Arizona. She was in charge of social media strategy for the firm and created, designed, and implemented strategy using Twitter, Facebook, and LinkedIn. Cali was responsible for curating articles and essays from the finance world and writing for email marketing campaigns to help educate the firm's clients and provide them with timely and appropriate news and updates. Cali does not feel like she has a "solid grasp on finance," but she still believes she was an ideal candidate for this job. Why? With a history degree, she was able to immerse herself in the finance culture and "make valuable, often creative, suggestions regarding how we disseminate information to our clientele." She writes, "During my undergraduate courses, I learned to eschew my presentism and put on the shoes of historical actors. In a similar vein, I enter the all too foreign world of numbers and acronyms and must make sense of my surroundings." As with Sonia and Tony, Cali's study of history has helped her to synthesize large amounts of data into a "cohesive narrative." Cali gathers a great deal of information about markets and mortgages and investing and condenses the material "into easily digestible

5. John Fea, "So What CAN You Do with a History Major?—Part 23," *The Way of Improvement Leads Home* (blog), February 12, 2010, www.philipvickers fithian.com/2010/02/so-what-can-you-do-with-history-major_12.html.

snippets for the clients." She can confidently say that her years in the history classroom facilitated her success "in a territory as seemingly foreign as the past."[6]

Pursue a Career in Business

Believe it or not, most college history majors go into business, management, finance, and sales.[7] Bill is the director of operations at the largest textbook publishing company in the world. He is responsible for inventory management for the company's elementary and secondary school division. Bill leads a team that manages more than 800,000 different titles. He is always looking to hire history majors because "they think differently." As we have heard from others, historians are able to take pieces of information or data and present them in a way that empowers business executives in their day-to-day work. For example, Bill knows that he has more than two thousand copies of a physics textbook in the company warehouse. He calls this a "fact." His job is to turn these "facts" into "truths" that can be used to make business decisions. He needs people who can tell a story about that physics book. In this case, the book is one of the company's best sellers, yet it is stored in the back of the huge warehouse. The "truth" that Bill hopes his employees will decipher is that the book needs to be moved to the front of the warehouse so the company can reduce the time it takes to get it to the customer. Business majors, Bill notes, are very good at "digging up facts," but history majors are able to tell him how the various facts relate to one another.[8]

Bill is not the only one who sings the praises of history majors. I recently received a press release from Brian, the CEO of a large

6. John Fea, "So What CAN You Do with a History Major?—Part 33," *The Way of Improvement Leads Home* (blog), July 6, 2011, www.philipvickersfithian.com/2011/07/dispatches-from-graduate-school-part-33.html.

7. Anthony, P. Carnevale, Jeff Strohl, and Michelle Melton, "What's It Worth: The Economic Value of College Majors": Georgetown University Public Policy Institute Center on Education and the Workforce, May, 2011.

8. John Fea, "So What CAN You Do with a History Major?—Part 30," *The Way of Improvement Leads Home* (blog), October 26, 2010, www.philipvickersfithian.com/2010/10/so-what-can-you-do-with-history-major_26.html.

financial analysis company in Raleigh, North Carolina. I had never heard of this man or his company, but after doing some research I found out that, in addition to his role with this finance company, he is also a columnist for *Forbes Magazine*, a contributor to the *Wall Street Journal*, and a regular commentator on the Fox Business Channel and Bloomberg Television. He had been reading my series of posts on careers in history and decided to weigh in on the conversation. Here is part of what he wrote to me:

> Any good and well-rounded liberal arts education is a strong foundation for business. Ultimately, you have to be able to write, speak, and think. Still, for me, history is singularly the best discipline for success in business. In history, you learn and become immersed in why people and groups do things over an extended period of time. History validates that people and organizations act in clear, recognizable patterns. You also learn about human nature. Behavior becomes very predictable, which is vital to understand in business because you have to be able to anticipate how people will behave; you have to stay ahead of actions.[9]

It appears that more and more people in the corporate and business world are seeing the values of a liberal arts education, especially in the field of history.

Go into Sales

Katherine Brooks is the director of Liberal Arts Career Services at the University of Texas at Austin and the author of *You Majored in What? Mapping Your Path from Chaos to Career*, a book I highly recommend to all history majors.[10] In a recent interview, she told me the story of a former student who was a history major and had an interview with Hershey Corporation for a sales position. During the course of the interview, the student was asked how his

9. John Fea, "So What CAN You Do with a History Major?—Part 29," *The Way of Improvement Leads Home* (blog), October 20, 2010, www.philipvickers fithian.com/2010/10/so-what-can-you-do-with-history-major.html.
10. Katherine Brooks, *You Majored in What? Mapping Your Path from Chaos to Career* (New York: Viking, 2009).

history major related to a career in sales. He began to talk about his history courses, particularly a research methods course that required him to dig up obscure information about some aspect of the past. In the process, he presented himself as a person who paid attention to detail and was patient and determined. He then began to discuss, according to Brooks, "the history of some of the Hershey candy bar lines and how their sales (and survival or lack thereof) was determined by current/historical events." He explained that the Hershey Corporation did not suffer during the Great Depression because people, despite their hardships, were still able to buy a five-cent candy bar. He also knew that Hershey had produced candy bars that were part of the food rations allotted to World War II soldiers. In the end, this job candidate "explained how his knowledge of history and appreciation for the full picture of a product would enable him to better understand his customers and the needs they might have due to their situation." He got the job.[11]

Work in Television Sports

Whenever the Olympics roll around, I think about Amy. Amy is a passionate student of the past who directs the honors program at a small liberal arts college in New York, but every two years she works as the supervisor of the research room for NBC's coverage of the Olympic Games. Amy began her work with NBC and the Olympics at the Atlanta games in 1996. She was in graduate school at the time, studying the history of the black power movement at the Mexico City Olympics in 1968. The NBC research department heard about her work and asked her if she wanted to join the research team in Atlanta. According to Amy, they needed someone who could "think fast, write well, research creatively, and was desperate enough to work 45-hour days." Before she knew it, Amy was ensconced in an office in New York's "30 Rock" awash in Olympic facts—past and present. Today she leads a team of

11. John Fea, "So What CAN You Do with a History Major?—Part 26," *The Way of Improvement Leads Home* (blog), April 16, 2010, www.philipvickersfithian.com/2010/04/so-what-can-you-do-with-history-major.html.

geopolitical specialists, sports experts, linguists, and journalists. She and her colleagues know the name of every person who is carrying a flag in the Opening Ceremony, and they know "what could happen in every event before it happens, and how to find out whatever anyone else doesn't know." As a historian, Amy knows how to turn small details into a compelling story for NBC viewers. As she puts it, "The ability to think, write, speak, communicate, innovate, and create: that is history well done."[12]

Become a Filmmaker

Sarah is a former history major who currently works as a writer and documentary filmmaker. The biography listed on her website says it all:

> [Sarah's] passion for storytelling began when . . . [she] was a junior in college. While writing a research paper on serial killer Henry Lee Lucas and his still-unidentified victim "Orange Socks," [Sarah] learned that the victim's grave had never been marked. Once her paper was complete, [she] contacted the funeral home that had handled the woman's burial and arranged for a marker to be placed on her grave. This experience made [Sarah] realize that she could, through her pen, give a voice to people whom the public had long since forgotten.

In the course of her career, she has learned how to "handle complex, sometimes sensitive, situations with delicacy." She also learned how to examine all sides of an issue and how to present the information in such a way that the public is able to draw its own conclusions. Sarah makes documentary films about cultural life in the 1920s and has even started an e-zine (a web-based magazine) devoted to the culture of "flappers," young women in the 1920s known for their short skirts, bobbed hair, and rebellious spirit.

Sarah studied history in college because she found that she really "enjoyed telling other people's stories." She loved conducting

12. John Fea, "So What CAN You Do with a History Major?—Part 24," *The Way of Improvement Leads Home* (blog), February 15, 2010, www.philipvickers fithian.com/2010/02/so-what-can-you-do-with-history-major_15.html.

research about people's lives and "putting the puzzle pieces together." Sarah describes her career as a writer and filmmaker—which she works at from home while taking care of her young daughter—as occupying "a place in no-man's land, between academic writing and pure fandom." She loves biography and hopes that her work in this area is "both entertaining and informed." Sarah says that most Hollywood biographies "veer off into fanfic [fan fiction] territory" with "no research to back up any of these authors' claims." She treats the job of writing about another person's life as "serious business" that requires thorough research. Her training in history has taught her how to investigate the past and follow a paper trail until she finds the answers that she needs to produce a quality film. She encourages all history majors, whether they pursue graduate work in the field or not, to write history and not leave all the good biography and film projects to the communication majors![13]

Go into the Ministry

Layne is a local pastor who majored in history in college and encourages future ministers to do the same. During his first year in college, Layne felt a call to pastoral ministry. By studying history he became a more effective thinker, writer, and communicator and developed a broad perspective on life that he has found to be very helpful. Layne finds that many Christians crave, as he calls them, "black and white answers to life's difficult questions." Yet, as a student of the past, he knows that "history teaches us that life is marked by mystery," and that there is a lot more gray in life than black and white. His years in seminary gave him the necessary knowledge and skills in Bible, theology, philosophy, and pastoral practice, but his undergraduate degree provided him with a foundation for writing, thinking, and producing sermons. Layne interacts regularly with college students considering seminary. He encourages

---

13. John Fea, "So What CAN You Do with a History Major?—Part 22," *The Way of Improvement Leads Home* (blog), February 10, 2010, www.philipvickers fithian.com/2010/02/become-writer-and-documentary-film.html.

them to consider studying history or a similar discipline rather than pursuing a major in theology or biblical studies. Layne's study of history has stirred in him a love for the past and a love of learning that continue to strengthen his ministry to this day.[14]

Joe is also a pastor who majored in history as an undergraduate. He credits his patience as a leader to his studying the human experience as it has unfolded through time: "One cannot complete a history degree and dedicate many hours to study of the past and not become more patient with individuals, communities, societies, and the overall complexity of life." He also knows that the Christians in his congregation tell stories about God, community, and the wider world. "The stories we choose to tell about these things," Joe writes, "matter because they shape our present and our future." As a historian, he is always asking, "What story has been told or is being told, why are we telling that particular story, and how is that particular story being used to inspire relationships marked by faith, hope, and love?" As a Mennonite, and a proponent of Christian pacifism, Joe tells his congregation a story about a nonviolent God. Most of his congregation practices pacifism through nonresistance, but Joe and his leadership team wonder if Mennonites should be engaged in a less passive, and more active, form of peacemaking. He recently took to his pulpit to address this issue, asking his congregation why they have, over the years, come to embrace a story of nonresistance (over a form of active nonviolence). He asked them how the embrace of this story has come to define their religious community and how members live their faith in the world. As Joe puts it, "Without training in history, I'm not sure I would have the ability or confidence to get our congregation to wrestle with the stories we tell ourselves in the same way."[15]

14. John Fea, "So What CAN You Do with a History Major?—Part 19," *The Way of Improvement Leads Home* (blog), January 18, 2010, www.philipvickersfithian.com/2010/01/so-what-can-you-do-with-history-major_18.html.

15. John Fea, "So What CAN You Do with a History Major?—Part 41," *The Way of Improvement Leads Home* (blog), November 16, 2012, www.philipvickersfithian.com/2012/11/so-what-can-you-do-with-history-major.html.

Become a Doctor

Medical schools want history majors and other humanities majors. I recently heard John C. McConnell, the CEO of Wake Forest Baptist Medical Center, tell a group of career counselors and college administrators that a student does not have to major in premed to get accepted to medical school.[16] Consider the case of Ryan, a student at Washington State University. Ryan wanted to be a doctor, but he also had a passion for history. So he decided to pursue a major in history but made sure to take the science and math courses that he would need to get into medical school. Ryan graduated as an award-winning history undergraduate and the following fall enrolled in medical school at the University of Illinois. Medical schools around the country, according to a 2007 *Newsweek* article, are looking for well-rounded students who not only are strong academically in the sciences but also have learned to exemplify compassion and empathy for others—the kind of virtues that studying history can provide. The practice of medicine takes place in an increasingly complex world, and future doctors need to understand the world in order to perform at a high level. This requires seeing patients as "whole persons." Doctors who have studied the past tend to be good listeners, especially when interviewing patients about their medical history.[17]

Rebecca is a physician and a graduate of a Christian liberal arts college where she majored in history. She believes that her undergraduate major helped her to "stand out" when she applied to medical school. Rebecca loved history but knew that she would not have much time to study it when she got to medical school, so she decided to pursue it as a major. More than anything else, Rebecca's history education taught her discernment. She has learned to be critical of the things she reads in medical journals. She asks

16. See "The Current and Future World of Work" (panel, Rethinking Success Conference, Wake Forest University, April 12, 2012), www.youtube.com/watch?v=1qDI yio2Nlo&feature=youtu.be.

17. Sarah Kliff, "Well-Rounded Docs," *Newsweek*, September 10, 2007, available at http://saveksuhistory.wordpress.com/2007/09/06/newsweek-med-schools -seek-more-nonscience-students/.

questions about how the author of a given article has used evidence or situated a particular medical issue in a larger social and cultural context. The study of history has also made her a more "compassionate" health care provider. It has helped her to overcome her "cultural biases" and "stereotypes" about the people she treats.[18]

Pursue a Career in Criminal Justice

Why major in criminal justice when you can major in history? Brad is a police officer in Colorado Springs and has two degrees in history. While at first glance there seems to be little connection between the study of history and the work of a police officer, Brad reminds us that the majority of an officer's job consists of "documenting, recording, and preparing different cases and reports that may someday end up in court." Many police officers, according to Brad, have very poor writing skills. He credits his "history experience" for his ability to analyze a crime scene or write a report of a crime from various perspectives. He has become skilled at "sifting through witness statements," which he compares to interpreting primary source material. Brad's degree in history has given him a richer understanding of the diverse people that he deals with on a daily basis. "Of course it's a rare occasion when I need to be able to recall the events that led to the American Revolution or how Martin Luther and the other Reformers of the Protestant Reformation influenced religious history, but that doesn't mean that my degree has been worthless. Quite the contrary!"[19]

Summing Up

As a professor, I regularly meet with students in the midst of vocational crises. Just the other day, I was chatting with a student

18. "Careers in History: Medicine," interview with Dr. Rebecca Jansen, Calvin College website, www.calvin.edu/academic/history/careers/medical.html, accessed June 24, 2012.

19. John Fea, "So What CAN You Do with a History Major?—Part 5," *The Way of Improvement Leads Home* (blog), December 10, 2009, www.philipvickers fithian.com/2009/12/so-what-can-you-do-with-history-major_10.html.

who wants to switch majors from psychology to history. He loves history and really wants to study it, but he is worried about his job prospects. What did I say to him? First, I told him that job prospects are bad for everyone right now (our conversation took place in one of the worst economic downturns the country has faced in recent memory), so he was not alone. Second, I told him that the job market is constantly changing. Very, very few twentysomethings today are doing what they trained to do in college. Many will change careers multiple times in the next two decades. (One study has placed the number of job changes before retirement as high as eleven.[20]) As a result, majoring in history, a bedrock liberal arts discipline, will provide transferable skills that will serve him well as he navigates this ever-changing world. Katherine Brooks argues that the idea of finding a major that will lead to an ultimate and specific career does not conform to reality. She notes, "Art majors become lawyers, chemistry majors teach English in Korea, economics majors become veterinarians, religion majors work for MTV, and English majors become psychotherapists."[21] Third, I told him that he should think about what he wants to do with his life. Once he has a few options, he should work with his history department adviser to do everything possible to achieve his goals. Internships and professional development experiences are essential. If a student loves to study history but wants to eventually work in the CNN newsroom, then perhaps he or she should get a summer internship in the newsroom at a local television station. Our department recently had a history major who wanted to go into real estate. She spent her summer interning at a real estate office doing research on historic preservation laws.

But there are also larger issues that history teachers and professors, and school and college administrators, must confront if they want to be effective career counselors. For example, we must equip

20. Mark Roche, panelist for "A View from Liberal Arts Colleges" (Rethinking Success Conference, Wake Forest University, April 12, 2012), www.youtube.com /watch?v=yL5HL3gDQmE&feature=youtu.be.
21. "So What CAN You Do With a History Major?—Part Eight," The Way of Improvement Leads Home blog, December 15, 2009. http://www.philipvickers fithian.com/2009/12/so-what-can-you-do-with-history-major_15.html.

students to be confident in the skills that they have acquired as history majors. Millennials (American teens and twentysomethings) know how to communicate through texts and social media outlets, but they struggle with face-to-face networking and interviewing.[22] Like Tara, the student working in Malawi whose story I featured at the start of this chapter, history majors need to learn how to sell these skills to potential employers. I recently heard about a high school history teacher who told the parents of his students at an open house night that "I was a history major in college, and since you can't do anything with that major, I decided to teach." Don't get me wrong, we need history majors in the classroom, but this teacher obviously never thought deeply about the kinds of skills he developed through the study of history. Rather than apologizing to potential employers about being history majors, our students should enter job interviews boldly, discussing their abilities to write, communicate, construct narratives out of the small details, listen, empathize, analyze, and think critically. As Stanton Green, a humanities administrator notes, "People find jobs where they look for jobs."[23] We need to instill our students with confidence. The ability to do this must somehow be embedded in a history department curriculum.

To put this differently, I am convinced that the culture of history departments must change. History majors have a lot to offer society and the marketplace in a variety of fields, yet we tend to honor those students who go to graduate school in history, largely because we want them to be college history professors. We want them to be just like us. After all, imitation is the highest form of flattery. So we hold these students up as feathers in our caps—evidence that we are doing the right thing in educating them. I am not so sure that this is healthy. It is time that we develop a different kind of culture in our departments—a culture in which our model students are the ones who go into nonhistory or nonacademic fields where they can find meaningful and fulfilling work. What would happen if we

22. See "Understanding Today's Students" (panel, Rethinking Success Conference, Wake Forest University, April 12, 2012), www.youtube.com/watch?v=xTnB7aMqJ5A&feature=youtu.be.
23. Stanton Green, panelist for "A View from Liberal Arts Colleges."

celebrated our graduates getting jobs in the corporate or nonprofit world in the same way we celebrate their acceptance to graduate schools at Ivy League universities?

Finally, students can never go wrong in following their passions. I regularly encounter undergraduates—usually in their senior year or even at a graduation ceremony—who tell me how much they enjoyed their college history class and, if they had to do it all over, would have taken more history or perhaps even majored or minored in the field. They are passionate about the study of the past but chose to pursue a course of study that would help them find a job right out of college or help them make more money. But as Brooks writes, "It's hard to argue with that high a level of engagement in a subject—their passion will translate to better grades, better relationships with professors (for recommendations), and a better quality of life than pursuing something they aren't interested in just because it's 'practical.'"[24] Or as the Pulitzer Prize–winning historian Laurel Thatcher Ulrich writes,

> Your own instincts are a better guide than the words of your former teachers. The best clue to the future, though, is how you feel about what it is you do. Yes . . . jobs matter. As professionals we need to do more to advocate for history and to support one another in our work. But we also need to ask ourselves what it is that drives us to study, teach, and write. . . . For those infected with the need to discover the past, there will always be mysteries pulling us through digital or archival darkness. That is why people with tenure as well as those without continue to write. [The poet Billy] Collins admits that though poetry fills him with joy and with sorrow, "mostly poetry fills me / with the urge to write poetry, / to sit in the dark and wait for a little flame / to appear at the tip of my pencil." If you have discovered that flame, you will write history.[25]

So what can you do with a history major? For some, it doesn't really matter. Sometimes you just need to follow your passions, and the long-term payoff in terms of a happy and flourishing life will be great.

24. Fea, "So What CAN You Do With a History Major?—Part 26."
25. Laurel Thatcher Ulrich, "The Trouble with History," *Perspectives on History*, December 2009, www.historians.org/Perspectives/issues/2009/0912/0912pre1.cfm.

Epilogue

History and the Church

RECENTLY I WAS GIVING A LECTURE AT A CONFERENCE sponsored by Duke University on the role that the Bible played in the founding of the American republic. Much of the talk was based on material from my book *Was America Founded as a Christian Nation?*, so most of the discussion during the question-and-answer time was devoted to this question. In fact, about half of my audience was made up of students from Duke Divinity School who had read my book in their American Christianity course. About midway through the post-lecture conversation, a divinity school student stood up and asked me if I had any advice for him and the other future pastors in the room who were charged to educate Christians about whether America was founded as a Christian nation. Or as he put it, "How do we go out and faithfully teach people in the public . . . to be respectful about our history?"

It was a great question. As a young man with an obvious passion for the church, he was refreshingly naïve about the disciplinary boundaries academics have constructed to order the human experience. Academic historians rarely speak to public audiences like the group assembled in the lecture hall at Duke. Historians tend to be much more comfortable in the archive or nestled safely in their ivory towers. It is even rarer for an academic historian to engage the needs of the Christian church. As the early Christian scholar Tertullian once said, "What has Athens to do with Jerusalem?" How often does one find churches or other Christian organizations engaged in a public discussion of history? Yet this divinity school student was asking me to bring these three worlds—the public fascination with the past, the mission of the local church, and the academic study of history—into some kind of conversation that was intricately connected to his calling as a pastor. I have been thinking about his question ever since; what follows is a brief attempt at an answer. I think it is a fitting ending to a book devoted to the subject of historical thinking, Christian faith, and the historian's vocation. What are the responsibilities that Christian historians have in serving the church?[1]

Any discussion of the place of history in the church should begin with those who know a thing or two about the subject—academic historians who are Christians and have been professionally trained to study the past. Robert Tracy McKenzie (a historian who left a tenured position at a major research university—University of Washington—to chair the history department at a Christian liberal arts college—Wheaton College—partly out of a conviction to use his expertise to speak to the church) reminds us that too often conversations about the vocation of the Christian historian focus on his or her call to "labor within the academy," to the detriment of the Christian historian's responsibility to "labor within the church." As a result, Christian historians have left the work of explaining the past to those who are not prepared for the task. McKenzie describes walking through a couple of Christian bookstores and finding only one book devoted to American history—an anthology of historical sketches edited by Toby Mac and Michael Tait,

---

1. This question was posed to me at the Duke University "Bible in the Public Square Conference," September 10, 2012. A video of the session, including the question posed by the divinity school student, can be found at www.youtube.com /watch?v=v6SYyE0F1iQ.

members of the Christian rap group *dc Talk*.[2] I have no doubt that if McKenzie were to make his visit to a Christian bookstore today, he would find a copy of conservative Christian activist David Barton's *The Jefferson Lies*, a book that presents Thomas Jefferson as an evangelical Christian devoted to the abolition of slavery, or Barton's latest publication, *The Founders' Bible*, a work that intersperses the New American Standard translation of the Bible with quotes from America's founding fathers and interpretive essays by Barton on such topics as free-market capitalism, the founders' views on homosexuality, and "Islam's war on America."[3]

As we saw in chapter 2 of this book, the interest in the past is high among ordinary Americans. Christians spend millions of dollars every year on David Barton's books and DVDs, watch former child actor turned evangelical Christian Kirk Cameron search for the "true" spiritual roots of the American republic in his movie *Monumental*, or attend a church seminar or historical tour on America's Christian heritage.[4] Unfortunately, many of these attempts to present American history to the church are often filled with basic errors of fact and interpretation, or they are used to manipulate the past for the purpose of promoting a religious or political agenda in the present, an irresponsible use of the past that I have warned against earlier in this book.

2. Robert Tracy McKenzie, "Don't Forget the Church: Reflections on the Forgotten Dimension of Our Dual Calling," in *Confessing History: Explorations in Christian Faith and the Historian's Vocation*, ed. John Fea, Jay Green, and Eric Miller (Notre Dame, IN: University of Notre Dame Press, 2010), 280, 284.

3. David Barton, *The Jefferson Lies: Exposing the Myths You've Always Believed about Thomas Jefferson* (Nashville: Thomas Nelson, 2012); David Barton, *The Founders' Bible* (Newbury Park, CA: Shiloh Road, 2012), www.thefoundersbible.com. It is worth mentioning that Thomas Nelson ceased publication of *The Jefferson Lies* in August 2012, citing a loss of confidence in the historical accuracy of the book. See Thomas S. Kidd, "Lost Confidence," *World Magazine*, August 9, 2012, www.worldmag.com/2012/08/lost_confidence.

4. For Kirk Cameron's movie, see www.monumentalmovie.com. David Barton's organization, Wallbuilders, has effectively convinced millions of evangelicals that the United States is, and was founded as, a Christian nation. See www.wallbuilders.com. For a discussion of Barton and the debate over the role of faith in the American founding, see John Fea, *Was America Founded as a Christian Nation? A Historical Introduction* (Louisville: Westminster John Knox, 2011).

For example, many American Christians use the past for the purpose of "restoring," "reclaiming," or "taking back" America. The idea behind this rhetoric is that at some point in the past the United States was a more moral or Christian place. If Americans could only get back to these halcyon days, then the United States would be a much better place. Entire political campaigns are based on this understanding of history. During the 2012 presidential election, Mitt Romney produced a video titled "Restore America's Greatness." An organization called Restore America operates with a vision of "the restoration and preservation of America as one nation under God." A similar organization, Reclaiming America for Christ, has a mission of bringing forth a "revival of a backslidden nation." Glenn Beck stands before thousands of people in a football stadium in Dallas with historical artifacts from America's past and calls for a "Third Great Awakening"—a "restoration" of America as a more loving and benevolent place. A quick Google search of the words "restoring America" turns up dozens of organizations, crusades, and articles concerned with returning to a more spiritual or ethically sound nation.[5]

As a Christian, I am also concerned about the way God views the behavior of Americans and all humans. I want the United States and the world to be a more loving, benevolent, moral, and even Christian place. But as a historian, the language of "restoration," "reclaiming," or "taking back"—as it is used by many of my Christian conservative friends—does not make much sense to me. What America do those who use this language want to restore? The assumption is that America was somehow a moral or Christian place in an earlier age. Those who make this argument, on one level, are certainly correct. Our popular culture—movies, television, the internet—has become more coarse, inappropriate, and certainly less biblical over the course of the past fifty years. And

5. Mitt Romney, "Restore America's Greatness," video, January 2, 2012, www .youtube.com/watch?feature=player_embedded&v=hoo5xNmLJbg; for Restore America, see www.restoreamerica.org/; for Reclaiming America for Christ, see www .reclaimamericaforchrist.org/; for Beck's "Restoring Love Rally," see www.youtube .com/watch?v=oXCIdT021xo.

there are parts of the American past—the gradual advancement of democracy, the welcoming of immigrants in need of a home, the founders' commitment to civic responsibility, and the various fights against injustice—that are compatible with the teachings of Christianity and worthy of restoring or preserving. But to say that the United States was more ethical or Christian in an earlier era is a more complicated proposition than many political pundits and culture warriors make it out to be. If one were to advance the argument that early nineteenth-century America was more moral than twenty-first-century America and that we somehow need to return to the values of this bygone era, he or she would probably get a strong counterargument from an African American whose ancestors were enslaved during that period or from a Native American whose family was driven off their sacred burial and hunting grounds by the idea of Manifest Destiny. Do evangelical Christians really want to restore the era of the American founding when only about 17 percent of the colonial population attended church? A deeper understanding of the past would help Christians think twice before making ill-informed historical arguments when they enter the public square and also be more cautious before making impassioned pleas to "restore America."

Part of the responsibility for bringing a more thoughtful understanding of history to the church rests with historians, but too often those trained in the field are either too busy writing scholarly monographs that only a few other academics will read, or else too tired from teaching students and serving their academic institutions to do anything to reclaim the interpretive historical ground that they have surrendered to the cultural warriors. Christian historians know that there is a problem with the way the past is presented to the church, but they hope for a sort of academic "trickle-down effect." The ideas in their university-press published books will eventually reach the masses, and their students will permeate evangelical culture with more accurate and responsible views of the past. As Christian philosopher and educator Richard Mouw wrote in 1995, "Tens of thousands of young people in Christian evangelical colleges and seminaries are receiving a trickle-down effect from their professor's work. These are future laypeople."[6]

I am sympathetic to Mouw and those who hope for this scholarly trickle-down effect. I hope that my work will have some indirect influence on the public and the church, and I know that some of my students have been "salt and light" for the practice of good history in their religious communities. But I wonder how effective this approach has been in countering bad history with good history. As McKenzie notes, no more than 5 to 6 percent of American Christians have ever attended a Christian evangelical college. Allen Guelzo reminds us that Christian colleges affiliated with the Council of Christian Colleges and Universities represent less than 4 percent of the 3,600 colleges and universities in the United States. "To serve the remainder—that is to say, to serve the overwhelming majority of American Christians," McKenzie argues, "requires that we reach beyond the boundaries of the Christian college campus—indeed beyond the boundaries of the academy entirely."[7]

Consider historian Mark Noll's 1994 manifesto for Christian thinking, *The Scandal of the Evangelical Mind.*[8] Since the appearance of his book, an increasing number of Christian intellectuals have entered graduate schools; created venues, publications, and websites for the exchange of ideas; and pursued careers in public life informed by thoughtful political engagement. In his 2011 book, *Jesus Christ and the Life of the Mind,* Noll took stock of how the evangelical mind had fared in the wake of his landmark book. He noted that "serious problems continue to bedevil evangelical thinking," but he also saw signs of hope—renewed intellectual life at Christian colleges, Christian study centers at research universities, further dialogue between evangelical and Roman Catholic scholars, the influence of Christians in the broader academy, and the launch

6. Richard Mouw, "Scandal? A Forum on the Evangelical Mind," *Christianity Today* 39, August 14, 1995, 25.

7. McKenzie, "Don't Forget the Church," 283–84; Allen Guelzo, "Cracks in the Tower: A Closer Look at the Christian College Boom," *Books and Culture*, July/August 2005, www.booksandculture.com/articles/2005/julaug/5.28.html.

8. Mark Noll, *The Scandal of the Evangelical Mind* (Grand Rapids: Eerdmans, 1994).

of serious Christian periodicals. He concluded that the cultivation of an evangelical mind was still possible.[9]

The Scandal of the Evangelical Mind inspired an entire generation of young people to pursue a life of the mind as a legitimate Christian calling. Many of them—myself included—became historians. As a graduate student, I read Noll's book, and in the spring of 1997 I attended a conference at Wheaton College devoted to its argument. I was more convinced than ever that I, a first-generation college student and the son of working-class parents, could follow God on a path toward an intellectual life. But it seems that Noll's clarion call for a more learned evangelicalism has failed to penetrate the lives of local congregations. I would imagine that most individuals attending Christian churches, save a few here or there, have never heard the phrase "the scandal of the evangelical mind" or have never ready anything by Noll. This is not an indictment on Noll or the hundreds of Christian intellectuals who have followed his call. They have diagnosed the problem. It is now time to provide practical implementation.

In July 2011 I was invited to Arizona to participate in "Hot Summer Nights," a conversation and discussion series sponsored by an evangelical megachurch in the town of Gilbert. The plan was for a member of the congregation to interview me for one hour, and then I would take questions from the audience for thirty minutes. My book *Was America Founded as a Christian Nation?* would be the topic of conversation. One of the pastors told me in advance that "Hot Summer Nights" was a very popular event at the church. The previous summer the congregation hosted John McCain. Yet, despite the information, I must admit that I was quite shocked when a few hundred people packed into the church café. These Christians showed up on a July evening—a night in which Phoenix hosted the Major League Baseball All-Star Game—to learn about history! I was impressed. The interviewer for the evening was Steve, a prominent Phoenix attorney and businessman. While I was

9. Mark Noll, *Jesus Christ and the Life of the Mind* (Grand Rapids: Eerdmans, 2011), 151–67.

a bit skeptical about discussing American history with someone from the business world, Steve turned out to be the perfect inquisitor. A devout evangelical Christian and a graduate of Princeton University's Woodrow Wilson School of Public and International Affairs, Steve was more than up to the task. He began the interview by turning to the audience and asking, "How many of you believe that America was founded as a Christian nation?" Nearly every hand in the room went up. This was not a good sign. As a historian and author, I wanted my readers and the people seated in the café that evening to see that Steve's question defied an easy yes or no answer. Nevertheless, I had spoken to this kind of crowd before, and I was just about ready for anything. I smiled and settled in for what I thought would be a long night.

Steve handled the evening like a real professional. He questioned some of my assumptions but also gave me the freedom to elaborate on some of my book's central themes. There was even a "lightning round" in which Steve peppered me with questions and demanded short and concise answers. (Steve learned that "lightning rounds" do not work very well with historians, who make their living preaching the complexity and nuance of the past.) The question-and-answer session was spirited. I am not sure that everyone was happy with my historical approach to the subject, and a few members of the audience made this abundantly clear, but in general I left optimistic. I wanted my fellow evangelicals to see the value of historical thinking, and I think I largely succeeded. When I arrived home, someone asked me if it was worth it to fly all the way to Phoenix (from central Pennsylvania) to speak for one hour to a group of evangelicals about whether or not the United States was founded as a Christian nation. I answered with a resounding yes.

I have done many of these kinds of events in the past couple of years, and in the process I have learned that there are a lot of people who can't imagine that a fellow evangelical would have disagreements with the kind of history that folks like Barton and Cameron are selling. When evangelicals learn that such an alternative view of the founding of America exists, some of them are open to change. They begin to think about the relationship between Christianity and nationalism in a more nuanced way. I have seen it happen. I will admit that it does not happen as often as I would like, but it does happen. My hot summer night in Phoenix and the dozens of other talks and interviews I have given for *Was America Founded as a Christian Nation?* have forced me to rethink my vocation as a Christian, historian, and intellectual. I am now more convinced than ever that academics and scholars should be able to take their research and explain it to a popular audience in an enthusiastic and passionate way. This requires taking the time to leave the ivory tower, hitting the road and meeting people in all kinds of settings, and bringing knowledge and serious Christian thinking to real places and communities. Christian intellectuals should not be content with merely writing a thought-provoking essay in a magazine that very few people will read. Most ordinary evangelicals do not read *The New Yorker* or *The New Republic*. It is time for Christian scholars to be more democratic. If Christian intellectuals believe that our knowledge of history can help society and strengthen the church's witness in the world, then it is time to think differently about the audiences to which we are willing to speak. It is time to think about our vocations, at least in part, in terms of service to our communities and the kingdom of God.

I have been inspired by the people I have met along the way. In the course of my visits to church Sunday school classes, adult forums, special seminars, and even, on occasion, the pulpit, I have learned that there are a lot of Christians who are hungry for intellectual resources to help them think about how to engage the world. While the purpose of the church, of course, is to bring people into a closer relationship with God and others, it is also important that Christians understand the culture in which they hope to live out their faith. I am thus encouraged by the Christian community at St. Peter's United Methodist Church in Ocean City, New Jersey. This evangelical congregation recently invited me to deliver a Sunday morning sermon on Matthew 7:1–5 as employed by Abraham Lincoln in his Second Inaugural Address, and to offer a Saturday evening lecture on how the study of history can contribute to a more democratic and civil society (see chap. 6 above). I am also encouraged by the parishioners at First Presbyterian Church of Strasburg, Pennsylvania, who have started "First Forum," a monthly series on how to think Christianly in our twenty-first-century world. They kicked off the series with a discussion of religion and the American founding. And we need more churches like Faith Evangelical Free Church in Fort Collins, Colorado, who put together a two-day seminar on the history of American evangelicalism. The possibilities are endless for churches who want to engage the past responsibly. Knowledge of American history is essential for providing the context in which the church bears witness. Knowledge of world or global history offers the necessary context for the church's missionary activity in the world. And, of course, the study of church history will do wonders for helping a congregation understand its identity and roots.

I am also encouraged when I hear stories like those of Dudley Rutherford, the pastor of Shepherd of the Hills Church in Porter Ranch, California. In 2010 Rutherford sat down in front of a camera and told the inspiring story behind the writing of "The Star-Spangled Banner." He delivered a dramatic rendition of how American troops during the War of 1812 (which he confused with the American Revolution) defended Fort McHenry (which he repeatedly referred to as "Fort Henry") from an attack by the British navy positioned in the Chesapeake Bay. Immediately following the attack, a lawyer named Francis Scott Key, who had watched the battle from a British war vessel on which he was being detained, wrote a poem called "The Defense of Fort McHenry." The poem was eventually put to music, and we know it today as "The Star-Spangled Banner." It became the national anthem in 1916. Anyone familiar with "The Star-Spangled Banner" knows that this song was written in response to one of the most thrilling moments in American history. Key's depiction of the American flag standing amid the "rocket's red glare" and the "bombs bursting in air" should stir the hearts of any patriotic citizen. For evangelicals, the story has an additional layer of meaning. Key was a Christian who served for more than twenty-five years as the vice president of the American Bible Society.

Rutherford's video went viral. It received over 1.7 million You-Tube views. But there was one problem with the story that he told. Very little of it was historically accurate. In addition to describing the United States as "colonies" (the year was 1814, and the American Revolutionary War had ended thirty-one years earlier) and consistently getting the name of the fort wrong, Rutherford misread the British motives for bombing the fort (they wanted to capture it, not destroy it), overestimated the size of the British fleet in the Chesapeake Bay (they had eight or nine ships, not "hundreds of ships"), and assumed (wrongly) that there were women and children in the fort. One part of Rutherford's account almost seemed to confuse the bombing of Fort McHenry with the United States Marines' attack on Iwo Jima during World War II. He described soldiers trying to hold up the American flag in the midst of the British bombardment with "patriots' bodies" piled up around the flagpole. This makes for a great image, but in reality only about five soldiers died in the attack, and we have no evidence of such a flag-raising. Finally, Rutherford claimed that Key was inspired by the following words from George Washington: "The thing that separates the American Christian from every other person on earth is the fact that he would rather die on his feet, than live on his knees." Yet one would be hard-pressed to find the quote anywhere in Washington's collected writings.

Historians were quick to point out the flaws in Rutherford's video. Many saw this as just another attempt by evangelical Christians to distort history for the purpose of advancing their political and cultural agenda. It was easy to be cynical about Rutherford's flawed efforts at promoting American history. But then something refreshing happened. Faced with the reality that his video presentation was inaccurate, Rutherford apologized. And he did it boldly. He stared again into a camera, but this time he said that he was "deeply, deeply sorry for any misrepresentation of the original story" and admitted that he had lifted the story, without checking its accuracy, from an unnamed speaker who specialized in presenting Christian views of early American history. Rutherford's apology was sincere. He comes across as a man of integrity, character, and humility. He appears as a model of Christian civility and reconciliation. He eventually made a new video of "The Star-Spangled Banner" that is true to the historical record.[10] Such a video may not be as effective as the first one in getting his God-and-country message to his congregation, but Rutherford does not seem to care.[11]

Summing Up

We need more exchanges like the one that took place between historians of the War of 1812 and Pastor Dudley Rutherford. We need more Christians who are willing to work hard to use the past in an accurate and appropriate way. We also need more historians who are willing to go into churches and listen to people. As McKenzie exhorts, historians should strive to eliminate whatever barriers exist between them and their Christian audiences, find common ground with fellow Christians by affirming what they already know about the past, and speak in an accessible and nonprovoking manner.[12] This is easier said than done. Most historians don't have the time or inclination to do this kind of work, and most churches don't have an interest in carving out time to make it happen. I wonder just how much the Duke Divinity School student who asked me how to present history to his congregation will remember my advice when he finds himself in the midst of preaching weekly, conducting funerals and weddings, visiting the sick, counseling the distressed, and balancing the church budget.

Yet I remain convinced that history has much to offer us Christians. It is time for historians, teachers of history, and serious students of the past to be in the business of teaching the public how to think historically. Historians—as historians—need to bring the benefits of historical thinking to churches, parachurch

10. New video is available on YouTube at https://www.youtube.com/watch?v=6hZe8CPGA1E.

11. John Fea, "An Evangelical Pastor Gets a History Lesson," *Confessing History* (blog), January 12, 2011, www.patheos.com/Resources/Additional-Resources/Evangelical-Pastor-Gets-a-History-Lesson-John-Fea-01-12-2011.html.

12. McKenzie, "Don't Forget the Church," 290–95.

organizations, Christian schools, and homeschool groups. We should actively seek to share our wisdom and insight in a Sunday school class, from the pulpit, in our daughter's fifth-grade classroom, or during a special weeknight lecture at church or in a local coffeehouse or bookstore. We should be writing for general audiences and teaching the past not only because it offers civic literacy but also because it has the power to change our lives and the lives of those around us. In this world of "centers" and "institutes," there is certainly room for a "Center for American History and a Civil Society."[13] It could be staffed by a group of public scholars and intellectuals, students, and community members interested in working with school districts, conducting historical tours, and engaging congregations. In the process, they will teach people that sometimes understanding, listening, practicing hospitality, and exercising humility—virtues that one learns from studying history—may lead to a more civil, just, and benevolent society. I offer a proposal for such a center in the appendix of this book.

As McKenzie notes (and as I have elaborated on elsewhere), such a move toward engaging the people in the pew fits nicely with the way the entire historical profession is moving.[14] Over the course of the past several years, the American Historical Association (AHA), the most important organization of historians in the world, has challenged its members to connect with the larger public. Anthony Grafton, the outgoing president of the AHA, used his term in office to encourage historians to use the digital revolution as a way to communicate to nonacademic audiences, and also to urge graduate programs in history to prepare students for more than just academic jobs. The current president, William Cronon, writes columns in the association's magazine, *Perspectives on History*, exhorting historians to update Wikipedia entries and write in a manner that is accessible to the general public. James Banner, in his book *Being a Historian*, tells historians to take risks by writing in accessible prose, by not getting caught up in historiographical

13. See appendix.
14. McKenzie, "Don't Forget the Church," 286–87.

debates, and by treating readers of their work as "fellow citizens." Indeed, all of these calls from the larger profession resonate very well with the Christian historian's vocation to serve the church.[15]

As I told that divinity school student, while the primary role of Christians and the church is to bring the transforming power of the gospel to change lives and influence the culture, space for conversations about the past can help bring an end to the shouting matches and can strengthen the church's witness in the world.

15. John Fea, "Conference on Faith and History Wrap Up: Part One," *The Way of Improvement Leads Home* (blog), October 8, 2012, www.philipvickersfithian.com/2012/10/conference-on-faith-and-history-wrap-up.html; Fea, "Conference on Faith and History Wrap Up: Part Three," *The Way of Improvement Leads Home* (blog), October 10, 2012, www.philipvickersfithian.com/2012/10/conference-on-faith-and-history-wrap-up_10.html; Jennifer Howard, "A Conversation with a 'Luddite' Who Championed New Scholarly Directions for History," *Chronicle of Higher Education*, January 9, 2012, www.chronicle.com/article/A-Luddite-Who-Championed-New/130273/; Claire Potter, "History and the Politics of Scholarly Collaboration, Part I; Or, Why Anthony Grafton Is a Rock Star," *Tenured Radical* (blog of the *Chronicle of Higher Education*), December 19, 2011, www.chronicle.com/blognetwork/tenuredradical/2011/12/history-and-the-politics-of-scholarly-collaboration-part-i-or-why-anthony-grafton-is-a-rock-star/; Anthony T. Grafton and Jim Grossman, "No More Plan B: A Very Modest Proposal for Graduate Programs in History," *Perspectives on History*, October 2011, http://www.historians.org/perspectives/issues/2011/1110/1110pre1.cfm; William Cronon, "Scholarly Authority in a Wikified World," *Perspectives on History*, February 2012, www.historians.org/perspectives/issues/2012/1202/Scholarly-Authority-in-a-Wikified-World.cfm; William Cronon, "Professional Boredom," *Perspectives on History*, March 2012, www.historians.org/perspectives/issues/2012/1203/Professional-Boredom.cfm; James Banner, *Being a Historian: An Introduction to the Professional World of History* (New York: Cambridge University Press, 2012), 166.

Appendix

A Proposal for the Center for American History and a Civil Society

Rationale

Thomas Jefferson said that a "well informed citizenry is the only true repository of the public will." Yet we live in a twenty-first-century American society that is woefully ignorant of our shared history and culture. Instead of informed conversations rooted in our shared past and the ideas that have shaped this nation, public debate has turned toxic. Self-interest has polarized us to such an extent that reasonable discussion between those of different ideological persuasions seems nearly impossible. As a result, democratic society has become deficient. We have lost social trust, become preoccupied with our own "pursuits of happiness," isolated ourselves into ideological and political enclaves, and failed to think deeply about the common good. How might we overcome this cultural civil war? What might it take for us to enter the public square with humility and grace? A rigorous democratic culture requires that we bring our views to public life with conviction and precision. But it also requires that we do so with empathy and understanding for those with whom we differ. What would it take to bring a sense of social reconciliation to our troubled democratic life? I believe that the answers to these questions lie partially in the study of history. Therefore we propose the formation of the Center for American History and a Civil Society.

The mission of the Center for American History and a Civil Society is to foster civility, strengthen democracy, and serve the common good through the teaching and promotion of the American past.

The United States has always been a nation that has looked forward rather than backward. As a product of the eighteenth-century Enlightenment, America has attached itself to the train of progress. Since the first American historians began to write in the early years of the republic, the story has been told of the relentless efforts of ordinary people to break from the tyranny of the past. The French visitor Alexis de Tocqueville said it best in the 1830s when he described the connection between democratic individualism and historical amnesia:

> Not only does democracy make men forget their ancestors, but also clouds their view of their descendants and isolates them from their contemporaries. Each man is forever thrown back on himself alone, and there is danger that he may be shut up in the solitude of his own heart.[1]

Or consider the words of Walt Whitman in his tribute to nineteenth-century settlers in search of new land and new lives:

> All the past we leave behind;
> We debouch upon a newer, mightier world, varied world,
> Fresh and strong the world we seize, world of labor and
>   march,
> Pioneers! O Pioneers![2]

1. Alexis de Tocqueville, *Democracy in America*, vol. 2 (New York: Vintage Books, 1990), 99.
2. Walt Whitman, *Leaves of Grass: A Textual Variorum of the Printed Poems*, ed. Scully Bradley, Harold W. Blodgett, Arthur Golden, and William White, vol. 2, *Poems, 1860–1867* (New York: New York University Press, 1980), 475.

For many Americans the past is an endless stream of names, dates, and places. We all remember the high school history teacher who stood before the class and recited, in the words of historian Arnold Toynbee, "one damned thing after another."

Of course not everyone thinks this way about the past. One will always find history books near or at the top of the *New York Times* bestseller list (think David McCullough and Doris Kearns Goodwin). Historians Roy Rosenzweig and David Thelen have concluded that ordinary Americans are constantly engaged with the past by photographing events, preserving memories, and watching history-related television shows and films.[3] We buy software to trace our family history, take vacations to Gettysburg and Colonial Williamsburg, and collect memorabilia, such as old postcards and baseball cards.

If you ask the average history buff why the study of history is important, he or she will probably talk about its relevance to life today. This should not surprise us. It is our natural instinct to find something useful in the past. Indeed, if the past does not have any connection to the present, then why should we study it? The past inspires us, it helps us to see our common humanity with others who have lived before us, and it gives us a better understanding of our personal and civic identity.

Others want to use the past to make a point. They want to engage in what historian Bernard Bailyn has called "indoctrination by historical example." But if we are really interested in engaging in an honest and thorough understanding of the people who came before us, then we will encounter things that are unfamiliar or perhaps downright strange to our present-day sensibilities. As the novelist L. P. Hartley once wrote, "The past is a foreign country: they do things differently there." People once burned witches. People participated in human sacrifice. What if it is the very strangeness of the past that has the best potential to change our lives and cultivate the kind of virtues necessary for a thriving democratic society?

3. Roy Rosenzweig and David Thelen, *The Presence of the Past: Popular Uses of History in American Life* (New York: Columbia University Press, 1998).

For example, the past, when taught correctly, teaches us empathy, humility, selflessness, and hospitality. When we engage in the discipline of history and learn to think like historians, we lay aside our moral condemnations about a person, idea, or event in order to first understand it. This is the essence of intellectual hospitality—a much needed antidote to our current culture wars. By taking the time to listen to people from a "foreign country," we rid ourselves of the selfish quest to make the past serve our needs. The study of the past reminds us that we are not autonomous individuals but part of a human story that is larger than ourselves.

Vision

The mission of the Center for American History and a Civil Society would be carried out through the following programs.

Lectures and Speaking Engagements

The Center is particularly interested in reaching public audiences through lectures to civic organizations, libraries, historical societies, college campuses, schools, and churches. In addition, the Center will promote its own lecture series of nationally known American historians. The Center administration will select a historical theme and will invite historians who are experts on that particular subject to present a public lecture on a local campus or for a civic organization.

Workshops and Seminars for K–12 Educators

The Center will sponsor workshops and summer seminars devoted to both historical thinking and the content needs of teachers. It will recruit some of the best scholar-teachers available who have the capacity and gifts for working with history and social studies teachers. In addition, the Center will develop a roster of "master teachers" who will work with K–12 educators and collaborate with participating scholars on issues related to pedagogy. These scholars and master teachers will be hired as outside contractors to carry out this area of the Center's mission. The Center will also work closely with Christian high schools, both in the areas mentioned above and in the integration of faith and the study and teaching of the past. Every other year, a summer seminar will be devoted to Christian high school history teachers.

Workshops with Churches

Part of the mission of the Center will be to teach historical thinking skills and offer lessons in church and religious history to Christian congregations. The Center will sponsor and deliver content-based lectures, seminars, and workshops on local church history, American religious history, and the multiple ways in which the leadership of congregations can use their past to move forward in the present.

Historical Consulting

The Center will serve as a clearinghouse of experts on a host of topics in American history who can perform a variety of consulting roles for civic organizations, historical societies, churches, businesses, and local communities.

Summer Academies for High School Students and "College for a Day" Lectures

Each summer, the Center will gather some of the best high school students from around the country for an intensive seminar on historical thinking as it relates to a particular content area in American history. This academy will include lectures and conversations with the staff of the Center and other leading historians in the field, historical field trips, and opportunities for informal conversations and leisure. As part of the process, students will work on a research project of their own. The Center will also sponsor a similar academy for Christian history students who are interested in thinking about the relationship between the study of the past and their faith. These seminars will be similar to the high school seminars but will also have an additional "integration of faith and learning" component. In addition to summer activities, the Center will work closely with high school history departments through "College for a Day" lectures. This program will bring historians to high schools to present new research and provide an introduction to college-level topics and approaches.

Residential Workshops for Undergraduate History Majors

Similar to the high school academies mentioned above, the Center will gather undergraduate history majors for a week-long intensive program focused on historical thinking and a specific content area. This workshop will include lectures and discussions from the Center staff and other noted historians, field trips to historical sites, and time to work on a particular historical research project connected with the curriculum at their undergraduate institutions. A similar workshop will be held for Christian undergraduates who are studying history. It will include an "integration of history and faith" component and a more detailed focus on Christian intellectual discipleship and vocation within the context of historical thinking.

Historical Tours

As a way of bringing the past to an adult public audience, the Center will conduct a host of historical tours, beginning with sites on the Eastern seaboard and eventually expanding to other national historical sites. These tours will be fun and educational, but they will also be academically rigorous. They will be led by a noted historian with expertise on the site or the era the site represents. The tours will be conducted on a comfortable tour bus. Tours lasting more than one day will include hotel and food packages.

Radio Program and Podcast

The director of the Center or another staff member will host a weekly interview radio program in which he or she will interview the authors of new and forthcoming books in the field of American history. The program will first be distributed across the web via podcast with the goal of creating a professional program that would eventually be syndicated to radio stations across the country.

Social Media Content

The Center will create and operate a daily group blog devoted to American history–related topics. The blog will be a one-stop shop for history-related news, teaching strategies, book reviews, and opinion pieces. The Center will also have a significant presence on social media sites such as Facebook and Twitter.

Implementation

The Center for American History and a Civil Society is still in its planning and visionary stage. Conversations about the need for such a center and its viability have been discussed with members of the historical community, members of the clergy, and others familiar with the world of nonprofit organizations and social entrepreneurship. At the moment, the Center could develop in one of four ways:

1. As a Center sponsored by a college or university.
2. As a nonprofit organization run independently of a college or university.
3. As a business run with a social entrepreneurship focus.
4. Some combination of 1, 2, and 3.

How the Center develops will have a lot to do with the kind of start-up funds, grants, and so on that are needed to fulfill its mission. Ideally, the day-to-day operations of the Center will be run by a director and an assistant director, who will handle many of the details. But until that happens, the initial staffing of the Center will need to fall to the director, volunteers, and unpaid interns with a passion for and training in American history. Center staff will be added as it becomes financially feasible. Once the Center becomes a reality, a board of directors will be chosen to provide guidance to the Center. The board will include historians, other academics, clergy, educators, and community leaders interested in the mission of the Center. If the Center is connected to a college or university, half of the board's membership will consist of faculty and administrators from that institution.

There have been a few successful models for this kind of center. The Gilder Lehrman Institute of American History, for example, promotes the study of the American past, primarily through the seminars and workshops devoted to the professional development of teachers and the sponsoring of new scholarship in American history through fellowships, prizes, and awards. The C. V. Starr Center for the Study of the American Experience, associated with Washington College, promotes American history through public lectures and programming, the prestigious George Washington Book Prize, a residential scholars program, and opportunities for Washington College students to engage in the practice of public history. The Starr Center provides a model for how such a center could work in conjunction with a college or university. Both the Gilder Lehrman Institute and the Starr Center are in the business of bridging the gap between the academic world and the general public, but neither organization directs its efforts toward working with churches or other communities of faith. Therefore, the proposed Center for American History and a Civil Society is unique in that its mission is to educate both the public and the church.

Subject Index

Made in the USA
Las Vegas, NV
25 June 2021